AUGUSTE COMTE

Auguste Comte is widely acknowledged as the founder of the science of sociology and the 'Religion of Humanity'. In this fascinating study, the first major reassessment of Comte's sociology for many years, Mike Gane draws on recent scholarship and presents a new reading of this remarkable figure.

Comte's contributions to the history and philosophy of science have decisively influenced positive methodologies. He coined the term 'sociology' and gave it its first content, and he is renowned for having introduced the sociology of gender and emotion into sociology. What is less well known, however, is that Comte contributed to ethics, and indeed coined the word 'altruism'.

In this important work, Gane examines Comte's sociological vision and shows that because he thought sociology could and should be reflexive, encyclopaedic and utopian, he considered topics such as fetishism, polytheism, fate, love, and the relations between sociology, science, theology and culture.

This fascinating account of the birth of sociology fills what till now has been a considerable gap in the market for an accessible text on Comte, based on new research. Gane's work is an essential read for all sociologists and students of the discipline.

Mike Gane is Professor of Sociology at the Department of Social Sciences, Loughborough University. His teaching interests are in the sociology of power, gender, consumer culture and in theory. He has published widely on Durkheimian sociology, on Baudrillard, and has edited two collections on Foucault. His recent writings have concerned Comte, Marx, Mauss, Lyotard, Canguilhem, Baudrillard, Derrida and Virilio.

KEY SOCIOLOGISTS
Edited by PETER HAMILTON

Now reissued, this classic series provides students with concise and readable introductions to the work, life and influence of the great sociological thinkers. With individual volumes covering individual thinkers, from Emile Durkheim to Pierre Bourdieu, each author takes a distinct line, assessing the impact of these major figures on the discipline as well as the contemporary relevance of their work. These pocket-sized introductions will be ideal for both undergraduates and pre-university students alike, as well as for anyone with an interest in the thinkers who have shaped our time.

Series titles include:

EMILE DURKHEIM
Ken Thompson

THE FRANKFURT SCHOOL AND ITS CRITICS
Tom Bottomore

GEORG SIMMEL
David Frisby

MARX AND MARXISM
Peter Worsley

MAX WEBER
Frank Parkin

MICHEL FOUCAULT
Barry Smart

PIERRE BOURDIEU
Richard Jenkins

SIGMUND FREUD
Robert Bocock

ZYGMUNT BAUMAN
Tony Blackshaw

AUGUSTE COMTE
Mike Gane

AUGUSTE COMTE

MIKE GANE

Routledge
Taylor & Francis Group
LONDON AND NEW YORK

First published 2006
by Routledge
2 Park Square, Milton Park, Abingdon, Oxon OX14 4RN

Simultaneously published in the USA and Canada
by Routledge
270 Madison Ave, New York, NY 10016

Routledge is an imprint of the Taylor & Francis Group, an informa business

Typeset in Times New Roman by
HWA Text and Data Management Ltd, Tunbridge Wells
Printed and bound in Great Britain by
TJ International Ltd, Padstow, Cornwall

British Library Cataloguing in Publication Data
A catalogue record for this book is available from the British Library

Library of Congress Cataloging in Publication Data
A catalog record for this book has been requested

ISBN10: 0–415–38543–1 (hbk)
ISBN10: 0–415–38542–3 (pbk)

ISBN13: 978–0–415–38543–5 (hbk)
ISBN13: 978–0–415–38542–8 (pbk)

[I]f the novelty and difficulty of my creative task should compel me occasionally to desert my own logical precept, the warning I have now given will enable the reader to rectify any errors into which I may lapse. (Comte)

[H]is analysis of history, to which there is much to be added … we do not think likely ever, in its general features, [will ever be] superseded. (Mill [1865], 1961: 123–4)

Method from every point of view has a higher value than doctrine. (Comte)

The hermit … will doubt whether behind each of his caves there does not lie another deeper cave … an abyss behind every 'foundation'. (Nietzsche)

Table of Contents

Preface

My interest in conducting research into Comte's work began after I had written a book on Durkheim's sociological method in 1988 and decided to examine wider aspects of the work of nineteenth-century theorists, especially their work on gender. This resulted in a book on gender, theory and personal relationships (1993), in which there is a chapter on Comte. In reading Comte for that book I began to see how much of Durkheim's method was prefigured in earlier writings of the nineteenth century, and how much my earlier essay on Durkheim should have acknowledged this debt. I have tried to remedy this account in my recent study, *French Social Theory* (2003). Subsequently I have become interested in Comte's sociology more specifically, and it is in this book that I set off in search of the first 'sociology', and the fate of the sociological law Comte claimed to have discovered in a torrid few days in 1822. He presented his law in a number of short essays now often called the 'opuscules' in the following years, but a full presentation and demonstration of it had to wait to the final volumes of his *Course in Positive Philosophy* (1839–42). The law was called the law of the three states ('loi des trois états'), which he claimed provided the fundamental discovery of the object and the logic of a new science, thus founding modern sociology. My purpose is to search for the nature of the discovery itself (if there is one), and only comment on Auguste Comte himself as a person, where it seems necessary for contextualisation or explanation of the logic of his thought. I follow some of my analytic ideas into the work of his contemporaries and subsequent writings of sociologists to locate Comte's particular position in this discipline. Jean-Michel Berthelot (1991) argues that Comte's thought belongs to the prehistory of the modern discipline. But even in Michel Foucault's archaeology of the social sciences in the eighteenth and early nineteenth centuries Comte gets barely a mention, since for Foucault the real sources of the emerging social sciences lie elsewhere.

Thus we have here a peculiar case of exclusion of sociological positivism, of intellectual demotion verging on elimination from the record. In fact it is fifty years since W.J.H. Sprott said 'Comte's theory is nowadays but a museum piece' (1949: 159), a phrase repeated twenty years ago by Ralf Dahrendorf (in Mommsen and Osterhammel, 1987: 579). But in which museum is Comte's sociology on display? Perhaps one could point to the work of Ronald Fletcher, who in his notes to an edition of Comte's early writings (Comte, 1974a: 250), claimed that there was a continuing Comtean tradition in British sociology that could be found in the collection *The Science of Society and the Unity of Mankind* (Fletcher (ed.) 1974), but turning to the volume itself there are indeed no indications of this claim in the collection and few references to Comte. It is true that there were from 1951 a series of Auguste Comte Memorial Trust Lectures, established by the 'English Positivist Committee' (given by such writers as Isaiah Berlin, Morris Ginsberg, Gilbert Ryle, A.J. Ayer, and by Ronald Fletcher himself (1966)). I think it fair to say that this was not a 'tradition' in any coherent sense, and there is now no lineage to the small 'positivist movement' that once existed in Britain. Today, however, leading introductory books on social and sociological theory are now including Comte once again; witness, for example, those by Larry Ray, Ritzer, and Shilling and Mellors. The new *Journal of Classical Sociology* has carried a long review article called 'L'Effet Comte' by Thomas Kemple (2004, 4(3) 361–82), symptomatic and indicative of this new interest. Steve Fuller's *The New Sociological Imagination* (2006) places Comte centre stage.

Acknowledgements

There are many people I should thank for help in one way or another in relation to this book. My first encounters with Comte's work were as a student at Leicester University (lectures on Comte by Eric Dunning and Ilya Neustadt) in the mid-1960s where the influence of Norbert Elias was predominant but never unquestioned in a milieu which included Anthony Giddens, Terry Johnson, Barry Hindess, Christopher Bryant, Dave Chaney, Nicos Mouzelis and Mary MacIntosh. I also encountered a different Comte in the postgraduate milieu at the London School of Economics where I did my doctoral studies, and where I encountered the writings of Bachelard and Canguilhem (thanks particularly to Ben Brewster, Tony Cutler, Mike Radford, Greta Jones, Ted Benton, Paul Hirst, and to conversations with Stephen Gaukroger, Ernest Gellner, Imre Latakos, David Martin, Donald MacRae, Dominique Lecourt and Louis Althusser). I have subsequently taught courses where Comte has figured as a major topic and resource at Loughborough University, and I owe a debt to many students and staff members and visitors (particularly Mariam Fraser, Georges Salemohamed, Mike Pickering, Jim McGuigan, Dennis Smith, Michael Billig, Steve Brown, Leslie Sklair, Bruno Latour and Jean Baudrillard). I have presented papers on Comte to many university departments and at international conferences, and I would like to thank in particular those who contributed to discussions at Lancaster University (especially Scott Lash and Larry Ray), Leicester University (especially David Ashton, Joe Banks, Anne Witz and Jack Barbalet), a joint Sussex-Warwick seminar held at Sussex University (particularly Andrew Wernick, Charles Turner, Robert Fine and Peter Wagner), further events at Warwick (particularly Andrew Benjamin, Keith Ansell-Pearson, Claude Lefort and Slavoj Žižek), a Georges Canguilhem Conference held in London (particularly Paul Rabinow, François Delaporte and Michael Lynch). I owe a debt to the editor of *Renaissance and Modern Studies*, Colin Heywood, and to members of the editorial board of *Economy and Society*, especially Beverley Brown, Maxime Molyneux, Thomas Osborne, Ali Rattansi, Nikolas Rose, Grahame Thompson, Nigel Thrift, Tony Woodiwiss, Talal Asad, Frank Pearce and Sami Zubaida. The Centre for Durkheimian Studies at Oxford has held many stimulating workshops in which Comtean themes have been discussed in detail (particular thanks to Bill Pickering, Nick Allen, Willie Watts Miller, Josep Llobera, Susan Stedman Jones, Mike Hawkins, Kenneth Thompson, Philip Mellors, and guest speakers notably Jeffrey Alexander, Edward Tiryakian, Lionel Kochan and Jack Hayward). I also would like to thank participants at the Auguste Comte Bicentenial Colloques held in Paris in 1998 and the 2001 Cerisy-la-Salle Colloque, particularly Jasodhara Bagchi, Daniel Becquemont, Jean-Michel Berthelot, Laurent Clauzade, Juliette Grange, Johan Heilbron, Angèle Kremer-Marietti, Mary Pickering, Michel Bourdeau, Jean François Braunstein and Annie Petit. At other conferences I have had fruitful conversations on Comtean themes with Terry Wright (at Cork) and George Ritzer (at Brunel), and at one conference in Paris to an anonymous member of the audience who leant over to me and said quietly 'after Pierre Arnaud died there have been no true Comteans in France'. Finally I would like to thank Monique Arnaud, and my nephew Nicholas Gane for all kinds of helpful advice, encouragement, assistance and constructive disbelief. Everyone mentioned helped me in one way or another to find out the lie of the land, clarify and sharpen my ideas, but I am naturally in the end responsible for any mistakes of fact, conception or interpretation.

I would like to thank the many seminar and conference participants, but also a number of editors and publishers for permission to draw from various chapters and articles.

First the following papers given to seminars and conferences:

'Sociological Theory and Gender: Auguste Comte', Sociology Department, Leicester University (1991); 'Comte's Positivism as Science Fiction', Department of Sociology, Lancaster University (1994); 'Comte's Law of the Three States', Durkheim Studies Centre, Oxford (1994);

'Durkheim contre Comte', International Colloque, Bordeaux (1995); 'Comte and Durkheim's Concept of Social Pathology', Maison Française, Oxford (1996); 'Comte's Theory of Abnormal Social Forms', Oxford University (1998); 'Comte's Sociology', Centre for Critical Social Theory, Sussex University (1998); 'La Science Sociale', (Table Ronde), Comte Colloque Paris (1998); 'Fetishism in Comte's Social Theory', (Sociality/ Materiality Conference), Brunel University (1999); 'Variation vs Plurality in French Social Theory from Comte to Baudrillard', Warwick University (2000); 'L'État Metaphysique et sa Periodisation Interne', Colloque, Cerisy-la-Salle (2001); 'Into the Abyss. The First French Sociologists', Inaugural Lecture, Loughborough University (2002); 'French Sociology Today', Warwick University (2003).

And second the following chapters and articles:

'Unresolved Comte', *Economy and Society* (1994), vol. 24, 1, pp. 138–49; 'La Distinction du Normal et du Pathologique', in Borlandi *et al.* (eds) (1995), *Les Règles de la Méthode Sociologique*, Paris: L'Harmattan, pp. 185–205; 'Engendering the End of European History: Auguste Comte's Cult of Woman at the Heart of the Western Republic', *Renaissance and Modern Studies* (1996), vol. 39, pp. 15– 26; 'Canguilhem and the Problem of Pathology' (1998), *Economy and Society*, vol. 27, 2–3, pp. 298–312; 'Durkheim Contre Comte', in Cuin, H. (ed.), *La Méthode Durkheimienne d'un Siècle a l'Autre* (2000), Paris: Presses Universitaires de France, pp. 31–8; '"Reading Gender Futures", from Comte to Baudrillard', *Social Epistemology* (2001), vol. 14, 2, pp. 77–89; 'Normativity and Pathology', *Philosophy, Psychiatry and Psychology*, (2002) vol. 9, 4, pp. 313–16; Review of *Auguste Comte and the Religion of Humanity* (Wernick), *The Sociological Review* (2003), vol. 51, 2, pp. 288–90; 'Dans le Gouffre. Entre Science et Religion, les Premiers Sociologues Français', in Bourdeau, M., Braunstein, J. and Petit, A. (eds), *Auguste Comte Aujourd'hui* (2003), pp. 151–69; 'Introduction', in Mauss, M. *The Nature of Sociology*, Oxford: Berghahn Press (2005), pp. ix–xxii; 'Untamed', *The Semiotic Review* (2005), vol. 15, 1, pp. 7–9.

Abbreviations

CPP *Course in Positive Philosophy* (1975, 2 vols). I refer to this in the text as 'Course'.
SPP *System of Positive Polity* (1968, 4 vols). I refer to this work as 'System'.

NOTE ON TEXTS

There is an obvious problem today for those who choose to write on Comte: Comte's texts in English. Many of the translations are very old and indeed not good on the whole. Unfortunately more recent translations are not always better. Translators have often felt the need to 'improve' the texts by omission of key clauses or qualifying adjectives. The famous attempt by Harriet Martineau to condense Comte's six volume *Course in Positive Philosophy* may have aided popularisation in the nineteenth century, but it has meant that readers have had their text dumbed down to a considerable degree, especially its theoretical content. More recently, Margaret Clarke's translation of a selection from the Course changes the content by eliminating text – her words are that 'many of Comte's pleonasms and expletives – adjectives, adverbs, subordinate phrases, have been pruned away, as they are heavy in English and obscure rather than illuminate the thought' (in Comte, 1974c, Andreski (ed.), p. 6). An example: Comte's text, rendered literally, says, 'the present mental disorder is, in the last analysis, due to the simultaneous use of three radically incompatible philosophies ...' (1975, i, 39, Andreski (ed.), 1974: p. 38). Clarke has cut the word 'radically' thus flattening and weakening an absolutely key theoretical point. Thus even this non-condensed translation cannot be relied upon for fine accuracy. If we turn to an alternative translation, that of Frederick Ferré (1970) who translated the first two chapters of the Course only, we find the same passage translated as, 'the actual confusion of men's minds is at bottom due to the simultaneous employment of three radically incompatible philosophies' (p. 29). Here Comte's words, 'le désordre actuel des intelligences' are rendered 'actual confusion of mens' minds' which is probably more misleading than Clarke's 'present mental disorder', but at least the radical nature of the oppositions is registered. My aim in this book is to present a discussion of Comte's ideas that is as far as possible accessible to today's students. Thus, where possible, I give references to the texts available in English. But as I have very often had to alter a translation to bring out an essential theoretical point the references are to the place in which Comte's discussion can be found in English, not to the exact phrasing. In this way I have thus not used expressions such as 'translation modified' or 'amended'. It is always possible to locate the original French source and the site of the quotation in an English translation. There are, at the moment, many of Comte's works available in paperback in French, some with introductions and notes which I have found to be very useful. There is, however, no book in English or French which currently offers a reliable introduction to Comte's sociological thought.

1

An Introduction to Comte's Ideas

Comte assumed, like Marx, that the revolution in modern culture and society had not yet reached its final destination. The modern revolution could not be reduced to an account of the events leading up to July 1789 and the official outbreak of the French Revolution. Its roots, he argued, could be traced back to the late middle ages, and the course of the long revolution still had to be determined. All his works even his early essays, were composed with the intention of constructing the first adequate explanation of the long 'modern crisis' and of indicating how it might be ended. Although there is controversy about just how consistent Comte's thought was in working out his solution, there is no doubt that in a rather surprising way, he did complete the programme he set himself in his early twenties. He founded sociology as part of this larger project, that is he conceived sociology as the scientific base for philosophical and political reflections which could provide the doctrine of a new political power. The initial programme was written under the influence of Saint-Simon with whom he worked from 1817–1824. How much he owed to Saint-Simon is now not in doubt,[1] what is clear is that the ideas he inherited were given a radical unity and coherence, a new idiom, not found in the fragmentary essays of Saint-Simon. It seems very probable, as Comte claimed at a later date, that his early essays were read by strategically located members of the new intelligentsia which was beginning to come to terms with the effects of the revolution, the legacy of Napoleon, and the restored monarchy in France. Instead of reading the revolution as an aberration, the new interpretation situated the course of the revolution in the long perspective of a European cultural and social crisis dating back to the thirteenth century. This perspective became an obsessive *leitmotif* and came to preoccupy and eventually to influence every detail of Comte's thought and life.

In this chapter I present a first outline of Comte's ideas, one that is consistent with how his sociology is read today. It is a reading which the following chapters however will question in order to get to the inner driving dynamic of the sociology and the logic of his intellectual career.

THE CENTRAL IDEAS

Comte's general view of the crisis can be formulated briefly in this way: his thesis was that any adequate account of modernity had to begin with the social forms of medieval European Catholic Christendom, a form characterised by the separation and ascendancy of a spiritual authority (the papacy) over relatively divided temporal powers (kings and princes). European history has witnessed a fragmentation of this spiritual power and then its usurpation by the temporal powers opening into 'modernity'. Eventually the Catholic spiritual power was displaced and then virtually annihilated in the course of the French Revolution. The fundamental cause of this decline was not the rise of the critical philosophy of the Enlightenment, but the combined action of industrial and scientific civilisation. The critical doctrines of the eighteenth-century enlightenment philosophy demolished the theological and monarchical edifice, but were not suitable for the task of social reconstruction. He argued that there was an inevitable logic here: society could be seen to move from the theological state to the positive state with an intermediary state dominated by critical metaphysical ideas. The new social science that he called 'sociology' has as its central object of investigation this very movement – the progression of these three states of which it becomes itself an essential component of the final stage. Once discovered and confirmed, a new authority built on the new science can claim its legitimacy in a 'spiritual' practice which in effect realises and therefore verifies the prediction established in the scientific law bringing the history of metaphysical phase to an end.

This intellectual programme involved the following steps: the formation of a preparatory scaffolding (the positive philosophy based on understanding scientific methodology) for the construction of sociology, the founding moment of sociology itself, and the conversion of sociology into a social doctrine as the basis of a new spiritual power. This power will gradually recover the position of ascendancy which the Catholic Church once achieved over the temporal authorities in medieval Europe, but now on the basis of demonstrable and therefore incontestable knowledge. In order to found a sociology based on a new philosophy of science he constructed an immensely detailed account of the evolutionary logic of the sciences one by one and as a whole, arguing that their development not only followed a determined order: mathematics, astronomy, physics, chemistry, biology and then sociology, but that this order could be understood as a system of dependencies (for example astronomy depends on mathematics). He called the theory of the order of this system the encyclopaedic law of scientific development. It occupied the first half of the monumental study which occupied him from 1830–1842 called the *Course in Positive Philosophy*. This study is dominated by an attempt to develop the 'objective' scientific method as it emerges from the natural sciences. In his analysis he shows that each individual branch of knowledge one by one necessarily passes through the three states: theological, metaphysical (revolutionary crisis), and scientific (positive).

Once the process begins, each new science creates the conditions for the emergence of another until the system of knowledge reaches the biological sciences and when this logic was known it would be possible to construct a sociology consciously by applying certain rules drawn from the analysis of the way sciences were founded and developed. He argued it would be by modelling the new science on the holistic frame of biology that a sociology could find its place in the order of scientific disciplines. Comte's central idea was that society too was revolutionised in the same way, that is, by the same triumphant march of reason. So it must always be remembered that as far as European society was concerned, he believed that all the evidence pointed to the fact that – like the sequences of the sciences – it, like the system of the sciences, was on the threshold of the final state bringing the process to an end in a completed system. The final social breakthrough was imminent in France. He thought the correct and objective method entailed the following logic: first to discover the logic of the past, then that of the future and only then could the present state, an intermediate point, be determined. The future state was not a simple extrapolation of current trends, but a unique state to be understood theoretically in its own terms. This knowledge of the future was more soundly based even if it involved the use of fiction than any analysis beginning with the complexity of the current situation: his sociology was far from being what is currently stigmatised as 'positivistic' although he coined the term.

After completing the founding study of the law of the three states by 1842, his life and thought were deeply shaken by two events. The first was personal. In 1845 he began an intense emotional affair with Clotilde de Vaux, at her insistence platonic, which lasted until her death in 1846 at the age of thirty-two. The second event was the marked change in the social composition of French society and the experience of the revolution of 1848–1851, particularly the emergence of the proletariat as a political factor. In the 1840s Comte's method and conceptions went through considerable transformations. He rationalised his emotional life as a salutary purification and spiritualisation, and even before her death he transfigured 'Clotilde' into a saintly figure whose image he began to worship. Reassessing his own project on the basis of his brief encounter with Clotilde he argued that all attempts to solve the western crisis through reason and science alone only exacerbated it. Drawing on the proto-psychological science of phrenology, all intellectual reason, for him essentially masculine, could be effective in the human context only if guided by the moral and emotional superiority of love and affection, the essentially feminine side of Humanity. Comte took his own experience of the sublimation of physical love as a necessary process for all those trying to resolve the social and cultural transition of the three states. Instead of the politics that seemed to be promised in his early work, he later installed, after 1848, the maxims of Clotilde within a project for a new R eligion of Humanity in imitation not of the 'liberation of the flesh' as proclaimed by the Saint-Simonians in 1830, but in a new language of scientific fictions and abstract love.

When he came to work out the logical system of the new strategy, he conceived the new construction in the language of a 'subjective' method: the law of the three states was to be completed by adding from the point of view of the needs of humanity a theory of the emotions to the theory of science and industry. Crucial to an understanding of the shift in Comte's thinking is a recognition of the change in meaning of the word 'religion': in the first writings it meant theological in the broadest sense, in the second period writings it meant the work of establishing human unity in every sense (which sometimes meant that theology was not religious and atheism was). The final, third, state became, surprisingly, a combination of science and fetishistic practice and worship (he wanted at all costs to avoid in his new edifice the errors of theism and metaphysics, but many practices of the theological period were retained). The last period before his death in 1857 was taken up with the dramatisation of the transition to the final and highest stage of society. The key element in this vision was the completion of the sequence of the sciences with ethics making its entry as the final seventh science, and where the sciences become organised by a new priesthood extending its authority over the European states (that he advocated should be divided into small and relatively weak city states). In order to reach this final stage the dictatorship of the proletariat would purify economic life of the commercial spirit by exercising a new moral hegemony. Paris would become the spiritual centre of the new republic, a sacred city, and the remains of the key celebrities in the long formative drama of the three states would be re-interred there in vast memorial ceremonies. The new authority, based on a complete and harmonised system of scientific knowledge, would guarantee an era of peace and stability in rational time (he devised a new rational calendar to complete the revolution's project abandoned by Napoleon).

The experience of the 1848 revolution was significant in a number of ways to the final shape of Comte's thought. The Positivist Society which Comte formed at this time in opposition to the liberals and the communists was active in the political debate as a utopian sect, issuing its own diagnosis and prescription.[2] He concluded that it would be the political action of the proletariat which would realise the final breakthrough to the third and final state and thus its conversion to positivism was simply a matter of time and effort. He presented popularisations of astronomy to the public for many years and came to regard the proletariat as a 'tabula rasa' on which to write ideas of the new religion. He concluded also that the proletariat would not be seduced by ideas of parliamentary representation, a form stigmatised in his eyes as resting on deeply irrational metaphysical principles and destined to be replaced by scientifically organised political forms. He appealed to the proletariat as the principal moral arbiter in struggles for the independence of his newly proposed 'spiritual priesthood', that is the new intellectuals organised on the model of the Catholic hierarchy.

Comte's thoughts on the new society now departed strikingly from the secular socialism of his earliest writings. Against the revolutionary and communist visions of the transitory dictatorship of the proletariat to attain an egalitarian society, he argued that the positive doctrine also legitimates a period of proletarian dictatorship but to establish a new hierarchical social order: in the economy differences of wealth would remain, and the family would be characterised by a new separation of the sexes based on the moral ascendancy of women. He aimed to appeal to all sections of political opinion, radical and conservative, since he wanted to reveal precisely how each element fitted into a broad scheme of social progression towards a stable final social formation. These propositions were worked out in continuous outpourings in the years of positivism after 1848.

The geospatial vision adopted here was on the one hand specifically conceived as a way of tackling the inordinate and essentially over virilised power of the great nation states by reducing them to smaller units. On the other hand the way that spiritual power could be restored would be to reorganise it into an effective equivalent of a medieval European papacy. The objective was to find a way in which civil and international war would be made a thing of the past. Comte's example was the form in which disputes between Spain and Portugal had been settled by decisions of Pope Alexander VI (in 1493) because the ascendancy of the papacy was accepted throughout Europe. In this view modern wars in Europe were the result of the survival of the militaristic ethos, but were caused by the uncontrolled wills of competing states.

THEORY AND PROGRAMME

Essential to the Comtean vision is the idea that normal social order arises within a system of institutional counterweights, but structurally quite different from those to be found in the theories of Montesquieu, Tocqueville or later by Durkheim. His critique of the political powers in modern societies is that they have been formed in a series of usurpations, in some way perhaps all linked together: the temporal, national usurpation of the international spiritual power, the corrupting influence of commercial interest over craft and function, and masculine reason over the feminine power of love. Critical reason and liberty have also usurped scientific certainty and ethical duty. The purpose of the analysis of the long crisis was to find the key to and decisive protagonists of all these related crises in the opposition between theology and science, since both of these are forces capable of establishing the substantive content of social formations. Against these two forces and their social forms, the metaphysical formation is essentially indeterminate, is unable to give coherent content to its doctrines of rights and liberties, and is therefore inherently unstable, or inherently in permanent and purely negative revolt. He had great difficulty in deciding what was normal and abnormal about this long revolutionary transition, and the tendency of his thought was increasingly to reduce its significance from one of the great principal stages of the three state law to a passing transitory episode. This tendency is complemented by the attention given to divide the theological state into three: the stage of fetishism, of polytheism and of monotheism. In effect, he constructed an evolutionary chain of cultures: ancient Egyptian fetishism, ancient Greek and Roman polytheism, medieval Catholicism, European enlightenment metaphysical culture (driven by the fundamental force of scientific revolution), and the revolution in France which brings civilisation to the brink of the scientific or 'positive' polity.

Comte's thesis expresses this sequence within a new law working as a gigantic spatial and historical organiser. Curiously it unifies key sites of the conflicts of the Napoleonic period, even of Napoleon's own career (his battles in Egypt and across Europe to Paris), into a theatre of action. The scheme of the law of the three states I suggest can be read as both an attempt to legitimate the necessity of the revolution as a particular stage in a long-term sequence, as a critique of the aims and objectives of Napoleon in particular, but also as a critique of the ideology of the restoration after 1815, of parliamentary democracy, and of revolutionary communism. The new science of sociology and the order of 'sociocracy' (rule by sociologists), is an attempt to provide for the western republic the science and ideological synthesis that Napoleon should have put in place had he been rational. What was abnormal in his project in effect was the regrettable restoration of metaphysical and theological elements in the Napoleonic period – but said Comte the progressive movement could not be held up for long by the work of a single individual. Comte (like Cabet who even specified how many pairs of knickers colonists should take to utopia, Nauvoo (Pilbeam, 2000b: 500)), worked out in great detail the language of his utopia: the social structure of the western republic should be made up of seventy separate states. The ratio of proletarians to patricians will be 30:1. There will be seven members in each proletarian family. Even the number of rooms in the household is specified. He outlined the three-phased programme of the final transition as a passage through the episode of the proletarian dictatorship and predicted the dates of each phase.

Comte is just as radical in his proposal for a reorganisation of gender relations. Here his aim is to reverse the tendency to the debasement of love in western culture, and to deal with the new phenomenon of feminism and the demand for equality between the sexes. Comte poses this issue again historically as a problem of the debasement of the ideals of chivalry and courtly love of the medieval period. His aim is to restore some substance to the idealisation and purification which the medieval practice seems to inspire. He commends the principle of eternal widowhood (with certain limited exceptions which would have applied to Clotilde), and reasserts the value of the segregation of the sexes, as the way of raising the status of women and to maximise their moral influence over men. The woman however should obey the husband, but the latter should adopt the cult of woman and guardian angels. The radical hypothesis, however, is that all sexual relations in society should be replaced by a utopia of virgin motherhood. This utopia would itself reverse the decline in the status of women and would give women complete control of human reproduction, the domestic sphere and early education.[3]

The specific details of the cult of woman were developed and practised by Comte: he specified as did the new religions of his period everything concerning the nature of the image, the prayers, the language, and the gestures in the cult's new rituals. The objective is purification and hygiene. What women will do is left as an open question to be developed and solved by women themselves in the framework of segregated and hierarchical structures, idealisation and duty. In effect therefore the Comtean programme for the family is intended to end the conflictual metaphysical phase within the domestic sphere.

Once the final stage is achieved the development of science itself comes to an end in a system of harmonised laws which are all conscious of their place in the totality. It seems at that point that life will return to a round of rituals, gift exchange, games, ceremonials, poetic re-enactments and reproductions of the various aspects of the three state law now become a kind of 'gay science'. In this sense the law seems to reflect Comte's own deep longing that the pain of the long modern crisis be ended as it predicts with certainty a future in which everything will find its rightful place. He noted in 1852 that it is the power of feeling which is 'the sole existing preservative of Western society from a complete and irreparable dissolution.' Indeed 'since the close of the Middle Ages, the influence of women has been the sole though unacknowledged check on the moral evils attaching to the mental alienation towards which the West more and more tended, especially its centre – France'. He insisted that it is only when men begin to think under 'the inspiration of woman' can they 'bring synthesis into constant harmony with sympathy' in a peaceful world (1968, IV, 437).

Comte's programme in its overall shape was world historic and encyclopaedic. It was born in the specific circumstances of imperial France, and bears all the traces of world strategic calculation, comparable to that of Napoleon himself. What is striking is that in summarising and unifying knowledge in a scheme which tried to be as up to date as possible, Comte initiated a particular type of combination of psychology and sociology: he accepted phrenology as the most adequate representation of scientific psychology, although he recognised it was still a proto-science. This suited his purposes in a number of ways, and he tried to work out a system of phrenology which would overcome common objections. Indeed this active kind of intervention was one of the goals of positivism in its attempt to show that sciences benefited from mutual review and adjustment of method and content. His phrenological psychology therefore came more and more to mirror his sociology and his Religion of Humanity. It is not surprising that his understanding of the relations between the genders reflected fundamental divisions in the different types of brains of men and women, and verified in scientific investigation of his time. Comte connects this in a simple and direct fashion with reproductive function and anatomy (reflected in the different locations of sexual and maternal instincts) but draws the conclusion from his analysis that it is woman who has the 'highest type of the mutual influence of the cerebral and the bodily life.' This has been made possible in social development through the fact that she has been 'set free from the pressure of active life, and made more and more amenable to the influence of the emotions, especially of the sympathetic emotions'.[4] The Comtean system here furnishes a complete and harmonised gender-space system: the woman is separated from active life in order to develop the highest form of physical and moral unity. Against egalitarianism and bourgeois elitism, Comte opted for a rarely understood alternative which might be termed a modernised estate system: a neo-clergy in charge of the moral order, a patrician order in charge of economic and industrial life, a proletariat and a matriarchy in the domestic sphere. The difference between this scheme and the totalitarian regimes that have borne some similarities to it is that Comte insists on the permanent separation and moral hegemony of the new 'spiritual power'. It is a 'sociocracy'.

The real function of the discussion of the future state was to establish the possibility of an analysis of the present. It is clear that Comte's peculiar inventiveness enabled him to undertake a number of different projects which are under discussion again today. He is a major futurologist. He established an important sociology of the emotions. But he was also a major historical sociologist whose basic theory and analysis is today almost completely overlooked, yet it seems that here there is a very useful sociological ideal type. It has not been developed within sociology except in now forgotten texts (Harp, 1995). In a sense this is partly an effect of the very style and form of Comte's own work as utopian fantasy tends to disguise the fact that the central aim of this imaginative construction is to provide an analysis of his own epoch and its crises by comparison with a future ideal polity.

In 1853, Comte returned to the great western transition and again treated it in terms of the contrapuntal movements of its main phases. But the reorganisation of his explanatory forms did not change: he simply added a note at the beginning of the story indicating the fundamental but passive influence of women – women preserved society from complete dissolution. He began to add his own life events into his sociology especially the decisive influence of Clotilde to the reconstruction of the positive philosophy. Nevertheless the social topography of Comte's later vision was strikingly different from the earlier one: the western revolution is an interregnum between two social systems in which the feminine principle, love, rules the masculine principle, the intellect. More and more the abstract systems at both ends of the historical sequence became structurally identical. The structures of the Catholic Middle Ages would re-emerge with the re-born priesthood of the new Religion of Humanity, a religion without theology and a philosophy without metaphysics. Paris would replace Rome as the sacred heart of Europe, and Clotilde would replace Mary in religious iconography.

ISSUES IN ASSESSING COMTE

In this chapter I have presented an initial picture of Comte's overall project and ideas. The early essays now seem naïve in proposing that it is only one more step in the direction of scientific enlightenment which will lead to the new utopia. The later essays seem characterised by long exercises in strange subjective utopian invention.

We may begin the analysis to be developed in this book from the following brief observations. Comte needed methodological inventiveness because he could not really use simple extrapolations. This is for two reasons. First he was faced with important oscillations in his historical sequences. Second he argued that such extrapolations were almost always misleading. He found a way around this by constructing ingenious ideas of primary forces (theology and science) and secondary effects. Modernity, the 'metaphysical' state, is replete with critical and negative phenomena, such as radical individualism, which are identified from theory, as normal transitory phenomena or as pathological processes affecting the articulation of social bonds. And above all he needed methodological justification for his final third state which he gave an idealised and purely imaginary unity in contrast with all he saw around him in the great disunity of the western crisis.

Now that the idea of the future utopia (in either its Comtean or Marxian form) seems so remote, it is probably a good time to examine how Comte used this part of his enterprise as an ideal type to look closely at what was actually taking place in his own society and ours. To do that there are fundamental steps that have to be taken order to clarify his notion of modernity (the metaphysical state) and the way he analysed it. In a Comtean perspective it seems evident that we are still in this state, indeed the third, positive future state seems no longer imminent, perhaps its last vestiges even disappeared with its twin utopia, communism.[5] Certainly Comte identified the parliamentary democratic state, and the doctrine of the sovereignty of the people as one of the principal metaphysical forms, and one subject to the vicissitudes of the inherently irresolvable tensions of that stage. But to pose this question is to bring to light a number of features of our present culture which are normally not at all immediately obvious to us.

The first is that very evidently we do not feel we live, as Comte, and Marx, imagined he did, on the verge, threshold of a final transition. There is no sense now in which the future seems more accessible to knowledge than the present, but many doubt whether the present is more accessible than the past. But Comte was insistent on this point. The present is confused and cannot be known scientifically except through the detour of the past and the future. Today sociologists can say with supreme confidence and without a second thought quite uncritically that 'we always know more about the present than the past (or certainly the future)' (Ritzer and Goodman, 2004: 92).

The second is that for over fifty years there has now emerged in Europe a sense that the oscillations of the revolutionary period are over.[6] Parliamentary democracies seem to have established themselves as relatively stable structures lodged in the European Union. These are not based on and do not derive their legitimacy from science, or social science. The sciences themselves have not formed themselves in to a system of knowledge with sociology at the apex, and social philosophy no longer sees itself as playing the role of harmonising knowledge into a coherent system. Yet Comte was insistent that the scientific enterprise is a single interdependent whole, and is understood as a driving force of the revolution of modern civilisation.

The third is a greater recognition that the revolution in the relations between the sexes is part of the modern crisis. Comte's solution of segregation and veneration seems to have been lost, officially, to the democratic process. But again Comte was insistent that the long traditions of specialisation of intellect and technicality in a reconstructed masculinity and of emotion and feeling in femininity will persist and, come what may, will continue to exercise their social effects. Comte was not in favour of breaking down this separation of function but of trying to reorganise it into a stable unchanging form.

Fourth, the nation state remains an element in modern political culture as a force which is still largely uncontrolled. International institutions have not been successful in developing an alternative mode of authority over them. The European Union could be regarded as having taken some of the steps towards integration, but not in the way in which Comte thought essential for the establishment of peace and stability; the resulting union cannot end the revolutionary impetus unless the metaphysical state has invented a mechanism for containing the more basic antagonistic forces.

Is the Comtean notion of the metaphysical state still pertinent? In the disciplines which think of themselves as 'social sciences', there is very much still a sense in which the object of their analysis is social development and progression. At the very heart of these disciplines is a deep sense that the evolutionary framework is still relevant, and that the post-modern 'incredulity' before grand narratives is dangerous. Even those who have attempted to write in terms of a post-modern problematic still find their ideas haunted by progressive frameworks (that is, they are post-). But those who want to escape both sides of this equation find their route leads to the notion of compromise between the forces of enlightenment, technical progress and science on the one hand, and the doctrines of popular sovereignty and meritocratic hierarchy on the other that constitute together the essence of the metaphysical polity. If Comte did not envisage the scenario that this compromise could become relatively stable, or that the third, state of positivity would join up with evolved metaphysical forms, it is certainly conceivable as a possible variation of his law of the three states.

It seems clear that Comte wrote in more than one sociological mode, and that a positive sociology might divide into more than one form of inquiry. Far from the caricature of a simple obsessive empiricism and drive to accumulate 'facts', Comte's sociologies cannot be understood without their emphasis on theory, hypothesis, fiction, and imagination which in the end quite overwhelmed the initial limitations of the research programme. The thesis developed in the rest of this book is that there is also a considerable difference between what Comte often said he was doing, what he said he had discovered and what he actually discovered, between the interior logic of his investigations and the framework of his basic law, and between the formulaic idioms and the terms of his radical sociological discourse. Looked at this way the overview presented in this chapter is both an adequate representation of the way Comte's sociology is understood by sociologists today, and at the same time a version of Comte's ideas which will be questioned in the following chapters. By the end of the book a different and more challenging sociology emerges. This new interpretation is in line with the historical shift in reading Comte over the last fifty years – from a period dominated by well-known thinkers like Aron, Kolakowski, Manuel, Popper, Hayek, Elias, and Evans-Pritchard,[7] to those, perhaps lesser known, but who have transformed the study of Comte today: Terence Wright, Mary Pickering, David Hesse, Robert Scharff, Gillis Harp, and Andrew Wernick.[8]

2

The Comtean Illusion

Auguste Comte was a remarkable figure. Loved or loathed, like Dali's liquid modernity in 'The Persistence of Memory' no one who has heard of his utopian schemes and his imagined place in them can ever forget them. Contributions which lie on the continuum between the brilliantly inventive and genial to the absurd have a power of resistance, because as Claude Lefort once said, 'absurdity is stubborn' (1988: 263). He is of course well known as being the founder of sociology in the sense that he coined the word and gave it its first content, the so-called 'law of the three states'. He is also widely known for his important position in the history of philosophy as one of the key founders of positivist philosophy, even if his own position on positivism which differs from later logical positivism is not now widely understood at all in its own right. He was a major figure in the history of science, prefiguring the work of Bachelard and Serres, and Kuhn and Laudan. He played an important role in the early formation of biology as a science. He was the founder of a cult, the Religion of Humanity. He played an important role with Emile Littré, in the production of dictionaries (of science, medicine – forerunners of *The Littré* – the standard French dictionary). But it is also known that Comte contributed to ethics, and indeed coined the word 'altruism'.[1] He is also known for having introduced into sociology, the sociology of gender and the emotions. Why, however, has there been an uneven relation, ups and downs of fashion, in relation to Comte's work?

This book on Auguste Comte presents a new reading and new assessment starting with the outline in the previous chapter as a baseline. This involves a number of different elements. First it attempts to provide a new introduction to the contexts of Comte's career. Second, it attempts to break into these 'sealed' classics, not simply to reproduce their formulaic structures. Here there are two linked problems, theory and method on the one hand, and substantive analyses on the other. I approach these issues by asking the question: why did Comte need to invent (or discover) sociology? What were the questions he was asking, and why these questions? Why did he need a scientific methodology and philosophy? How does his approach to the sciences lead him to a theory of the harmonisation of knowledge through positive philosophy? How would this be achieved? What are the intellectual links between this project and the project for the political form of the positive stage of history?

OPENING UP COMTEAN THEORY

My reading of Comte does not assume because some idea appears bizarre, even that there is 'lunacy' (Evans-Pritchard) in his later works, that Comte must be exhibiting signs of some mental illness. Apart from the very specific period in which he certainly had a breakdown in 1826–1827, he was quite sane. Psychoanalysts have pronounced on Comte of course. But their conclusions are crass: he was suffering from 'meglomania' (Fishman, 1950: 68). I take another route to the texts. Like Barthes this is not to return to a text in order to discover the secret madness of its content, but to release the author from the bond which enslaves the 'text from its purpose of guarantee' (to be Comtean) and to discover the 'happiness of writing' (even in melancholy) (Barthes, 1976: 9). The only way in which his utopia of the virgin mother can be read with profit today is to imagine that it was written by a Musil, Hermann Hesse, H.G. Wells, or even Salvador Dali or Michel Houellebecq.[2] All of Comte's fictions have the form of an imaginary experiment: they are virtual possibilities constructed to help analysis, and then sacrificed in the process of analysis. We might say that whereas the Borgesian labyrinth is enchanted and fantastic positivism, the Comtean encyclopedia is a closed enigma, since Comte was at pains to imprison the incipient strangeness of his visions in a perspective that went from an infinite universe to a closed world.

Certainly some readers cannot even accept the legitimacy of the move that Comte made in adopting the subjective method. Pickering notes for example that at a crucial point in his writing, 'he seemed to be getting lost in a useless accumulation of details. He appeared to be playing with his system, rearranging the parts, redefining his terms, and creating schema after schema for no apparent reason … His intellectual games suggest that his hold on reality was slipping' (Pickering, 1993: 686). Again, I suggest this judgement is too conservative and has to be resisted, since Comte was reconfiguring the relation between the theoretical and its relation to the 'real'.

The first attempt at interpretation must involve an attempt to determine just how idiosyncratic the idea is. In most cases it is very quickly evident that Comte is, in his own way, simply following something of a fashion of his own times that now seems to us bizarre (Charlton, 1963). In other instances where theoretical expressions are concerned, it often turns out that what to us looks idiosyncratic to Comte were terms in widespread usage in his period. He used expressions such as social physiology, criticised metaphysical entities (êtres) as mistakenly conceived as 'ontological'. Here he was in fact adopting, enthusiastically, the terms developed by Broussais whose 'Treatise on Irritation' he reviewed in 1828 (1998, 228–40; see Jan Goldstein 1990: 250). Comte's work is, as many have noted, marked by its continuous synthetic appropriations but these were quite different from 'eclecticism' of Victor Cousin who held to theology, metaphysics and science simultaneously (Brooks, 1998: 35–57; Goldstein, 2005: 139–232).

My reading then tends to follow Mike Hawkins and Andrew Wernick in the sense that although it is clear that for example phrenology is currently regarded as at best a 'proto-science' it is not to be overlooked as an important repertoire for Comte's theorising. Rather as some authors today seem to be able to manipulate Freudian terminology at will to suit their own purposes, Comte manipulated phrenology for his (Vernon, 1986). As long as this is openly acknowledged, it is clear where the reader stands. Not only does he declare his intentions when he begins to 'harmonise' sciences, and to order them, he is also very clear about the status of his propositions and conceptions. Although his method insists that all scientific propositions must be capable of demonstration with respect to observable phenomena, this does not prevent him from indulging in the most extreme forms of theoretical invention especially about future states. Propositions about future states do not violate his rule that science only deals with potentially demonstrable theory. And he insisted that the Religion of Humanity was demonstrable, not demonstrated. In fact this expression reflects to the letter Comte's epistemological thinking.

THE TEMPTATIONS OF A STRUCTURALIST READING

Certainly it is tempting to suggest that the works of the two periods of his intellectual life should be read differently. In the first the most appropriate would be a mode of reading such that a symptomatic reading developed by structuralists. This would be particularly sensitive to the epistemological novelty of Comte's new positive idiom, yet not be bound by the manifest order of the surface of these texts. Althusser for example has written of the way that a science 'can only pose problems on the terrain and within the horizon of a definite theoretical structure, its problematic, which constitutes its absolute and definite condition of possibility, and hence the absolute determination of the forms in which all problems must be posed, at any given moment in the science' and Althusser adds 'Comte often came very close to this idea.' Here there is no longer an individual subject with a vision, and vision 'loses the religious privileges of divine reading' (in Althusser and Balibar, 1970: 25).

Clearly both Marx and Comte present new kinds of social analysis and explanation: Marx has a theory of hidden, or in Althusser's term, absent causes (also of course to be found in psychoanalysis and the theory of the unconscious); Comte tries to eliminate causes in his epistemology but in fact enunciates in his account something very close to a structural analysis.

First we might look at Marx's notion of a real process that can explain the contents of historical consciousness:

> It is not the consciousness of men that determines their existence, but their social existence that determines their consciousness … it is always necessary to distinguish between the material transformation of the economic conditions of production, which can be determined with the precision of natural science, and the legal, political, religious, artistic or philosophic – in short ideological forms in which men become conscious of this conflict and fight it out. Just as one does not judge an individual by what he thinks about himself, so one cannot judge a period of transformation by its consciousness, but, on the contrary, this consciousness must be explained from the conflict existing between the social forces of production and the relations of production.
>
> (Marx, [1858] 1971: 21)

Marx has, then, a theory of the mode of production as determinant, and an evolutionist theory of the development of progressive stages of economic production: 'In broad outline, the Asiatic, ancient, feudal and modern bourgeois modes of production may be designated as epochs marking progress in the economic development of society' (1971: 21). The problem for Marx was to justify the contention that this was a series governed by a single law, and that the series was indeed progressive. In fact Marxists have never succeeded at explaining the 'progressive' sequence of modes of production, and struggle to explain the transition from capitalism to communism as a law-governed process. Althusser tried to develop a theory of conjunctural complexity, inventing the concepts of structural causality, and metonymic causality (part to whole) which takes from Freud the principle of overdetermination. But, in the main, Marxism remained wedded to the principle of economic determination and a theory of the progressive sequence of modes of production, without having a principle or a general law of this sequence.

These problems do not arise for Comte. His law of the three states is a law governing the development of all societies apparently through a single series (theological, metaphysical, and positive). It is progressive in the sense that it is governed directly and indirectly by increasing rationalisation and knowledge (the development of the sciences and technology). He wants to discover a certain kind of law (a correlation, either static or dynamic), but he then has to provide a theorisation since a genuine law is not merely an empirical accumulation. Far from being an empiricist, he regards abstraction and theory as essential to all cultures at all times, and developed in a particular way in the sciences as they develop into a system. In fact, he rejects all notions of causation in science as metaphysical, his social analysis does resemble that of Marx, for the element which governs social development is clearly intellectual progress.

But if Marx refers to an element as determining, specifically the material process of production determines the ideological superstructure his analysis examines consciousness as ways in which this superstructure is the place in which the conflicts arising elsewhere are fought out. How does Comte deal with this issue? In fact he deals with it in a very similar way. He analyses his progressive stages by examining the degree of development of the sciences on the one hand, but also the degree to which rationalisation of the elements of the culture have taken place. If we look at this in terms of the various activities in a society, Comte examines the internal evolution of the religious culture in his two famous sequences: one religious, fetishism, polytheism, monotheism and so on, and one scientific, mathematics, astronomy, physics, chemistry, biology, sociology. What is the relationship between the two series? Comte is clear that the driving force is the progression of the latter series. The development of the metaphysical stage depends on the development of positivism and is not a realisation of the pure logic of metaphysical criticism. But he does not say that therefore positivist movement is a hidden cause, and his whole concept of scientific explanation would prevent him from adopting this kind of expression.

In fact it is clear right from his early essays he was struggling to work out new ways of analysing social development. Here is an example from 1822:

> The fall of the feudal and theological system does not stem … from recent and so to speak accidental causes. Instead of being the effect of the crisis, it is on the contrary its source. The decline of this system has taken effect gradually over the preceding centuries, by a succession of modifications, to which, independent of any human will, all classes of society have contributed, and of which kings themselves have often been the primary agents or the most ardent promoters. It has been, in short, the necessary consequence of the course of civilisation.
>
> (1998: 51)

Although Comte critiqued the metaphysical notion of substantive cause, causes emanating from vague entities, or wills, he still uses the word and the concept throughout his writings. Even in the passage I have cited it is clear that he uses the word 'agent' in a very active sense, distinguishing between primary and secondary agents.[4]

Althusser believed Marx had established the scientific object of the social sciences as the science of social formations. Thus for him the crucial task was how to read Marx in order to show how the scientific breakthrough Marx had been achieved. This became for Althusser a theory of the epistemological break as class struggle in 'theory'. Rather than examine science and its laws in practice however Althusser was essentially interested in showing how Marx's theory embodied all the abstract characteristics and prerequisites of scientificity, and how this differed from prescientific knowledge (that is knowledge prior to the epistemological break) through the impulsion of proletarian perspectives. Althusser's interpretation of the development of social theory would argue that in its Comtean and Durkheimian form, sociology is developed primarily within the orbit of a class culture and this decisively influenced, even determined, the way it developed. By the late 1970s he had changed his view to one closer to that of Foucault which held that Marx had only provided a first critique of 'political economy' a science which belonged to a nineteenth century *episteme*. In fact Derrida noted, adopting terms strangely reminiscent of Comte's underestimated critical theory, there was throughout a dependence on the primacy of the 'economic' that was perhaps the 'metaphysical anchoring' of the whole Marxian theoretical edifice (in Kaplan, 1993: 204). Comte was evidently trying to eliminate any such metaphysics in his system and went to very considerable lengths to prevent it re-emerging as did Marx, but both theorists engage in similar ways with messianic time and the completion of a promise hidden away in the structures of history.

THE TEMPTATION OF A FATAL READING

Another of the central difficulties in any overall assessment of Comte's work is that for the most part interpretation cannot accept a place for the subjective method within the framework of modern science, and Comte seems to have confirmed this in designating the final works as 'instituting the Religion of Humanity' on the basis of a subjective reading of the new science of sociology. The significance of the later analysis as complementing and going beyond an objective method is important, since Comte did not, even in his so-called 'madness,' ever confuse the two. His argument is that all the attempts that have been made to unite the objective sciences into a single whole in their substance had failed. Such unity could only be achieved from a human point of view. What seems to happen in this case, as in others we will encounter, is that when the moment of radical objectivity is relaxed or acts at a distance, the imagination encounters again in new conditions all that which had previously been stigmatised as 'superstition'.

Perhaps it is time, then, to read Comte's late work from a different point of view from that of the rationalists or to read from a number of different points of view? After all, as Edward Said has pointed out in reading the history of Islam, for Renan, a historian who had taken on board important elements of positivism (he said that that the law of the three states was 'a formula that was true in the main' ([1848] 1890: 513)), 'language and culture were to be treated by philology in a temporal perspective, as aspects of a typology of historical periods'. While in contrast 'Massignon tries to experience the distance between Islam and Christianity, as a variant on the distance between man and God or between the word and spirit', Renan is the judge of lesser religions, but Massignon has a 'Christian compassion for Islam' which allows him to be the 'rarest-veined unraveler of Islamic civilisation the West has produced' (Said, 1984: 284, 288). Thus we might invoke an ironic turn and suggest readers who might play the role of Massignon in turn as post-modern readers of Comte. One of those might be Roland Barthes who called for a clairvoyant semiology. The reason for turning to a writer like Barthes is that here there is no simple return to theology, but rather, like Comte's own thought it follows on from and is a response to theoretical fetishism in modernity, and may provide a compassion for a particular language and experience (parallel to that of Massignon's for Islam). Roland Barthes suggests reading through the pleasures of the author, or more provocatively to identify in the violence of a text that which 'enables it to exceed the laws of that society' (Barthes 1976:10). It is not in its idiom of positivisation, or in its sentimental utopianism that Comte is excessive, but in the inner theoretical violence of Comte's project taken to extremes, that is visible to the eyes of Mill and of Littré, who wanted to construct a rational and liberal secular elite (Knights, 1978: 176).

In reading Comte it is perhaps important also to take into account what Baudrillard said about theory-fiction: 'what theory can do is to defy the world to be more: more objective ... It has meaning only in terms of this exorcism. The distance theory takes is not that of retreat, but of exorcism. It thus takes on the power of a fatal sign, even more inexorable than reality ...' (Baudrillard, 1988: 100). Umberto Eco also has a significant place for a text that can act as fatal symbolic power and so resist incorporation into a cannon (see Gane, 2005). These orientations are quite consistent with an attempt to intensify the neo-fetishism introduced by Comte into sociology. Comte tried to aestheticise his utopia, to present it as an idealisation in order for it to function theoretically as a rallying point for a cult, as well as to function as a sociological ideal-type. Instead of the brilliant crystalline forms of a celestial city imagined by a Calvino, it fell into the neo-gothic, and romantic sentimentalism (see Dijkstra, 1986: 31–3). Instead of holding himself at a distance like Hermann Hesse (1974: 152–4), he began to pontificate on all kinds of subjects and disputes. Some interpreters have seen this later Comte as even more radical than the first, an attempt to get to a genuinely 'post-modern' form of social analysis beyond the limitations of a narrow empirical positivism.

It is interesting to turn to Comte's own ideas on reading and writing in the subjective mode, as they are rich and radical, especially the futurological idealisations of the second period of his work. Comte argues that our own system of writing, derived from the theistic stage, will be replaced in the positive polity by a new form of algebraic writing. This would be writing in space, not on a material substance, and could be imagined as a green text on a white ground. John Stuart Mill's reaction to these post-modern ideas was scathing, calling them 'deplorable', 'strange conceits', a 'melancholy decadence' and 'ridiculous' (1961: 194f.). But had Mill really taken on board the full force of Comte's critique of the limits of pure rationalism? Mill seemed to think that the combination of positive science with a neo-fetishism an extension into decadence (rather in the same way that Comte himself comments on the 'vagaries' of the reflections of Newton in old age in his earlier work (1974b: 727)).

Littré too judged this a return to the theological state (see Charlton, 1959: 57–8), but again this is inaccurate, since the religion of Humanity combines elements from all the previous states including the metaphysical. Today there is widespread interest in fetishism, from Maffesoli to Baudrillard, from Serres to Latour, and a counter-critique which mirrors that of 150 years ago by Mill and Littré notably that by Sokal and Bricmont (1998).

But few have dared to venture the idea of a new religion based on scientific findings except perhaps in the vein of Edward O. Wilson who advocates that we 'close the tectonic gap between science and faith-based religion … [though] a humanism based on science … the light and the way at last placed before us'.[5] E.O. Wilson gets his inspiration from the idea of concilience from William Whewell the English historian of science whose work formed an alternative to that of Comte in the 1840s. But as Jay Gould has pointed out Whewell did not admit the extension of conscience into the study of life, and even rejected Darwin. Logically Wilson is more Comtean than Whewellian. But the phrase 'religion of humanity' can be found in the writings of the French metaphysical thinkers of the eighteenth century, for example famously in Rousseau's *Social Contract*: 'the religion of humanity … not the Christianity of today, but of the Gospel …Under this holy, sublime and true religion, men, as children of the same God, look on all others as brothers' (Rousseau, 1968: 182). Comte turns the 'religion of humanity', meaning perhaps merely belonging to humanity, into the 'religion of Humanity' a religion which worships Humanity, a new type of Supreme Being. Comte here is a creator of a completely new concept and language of 'religion' (one that later sociologists like Durkheim largely misunderstood), which Barthes terms as 'logothete', who says in effect the loss of the metaphysical world is a loss that must be registered in a new language 'in order to become unconditional' (Barthes, 1976: 5). Comte is the Calvin of scientific humanism but without the charisma.

THE COMTEAN ILLUSION DEFINED

In reading Comte and his interpreters I have become increasingly distrustful of formulas. At a certain point I became aware that Comte's law of the three states could be read as a law of two states, or a law of five or six states, depending on the stage of Comte's own thinking. Or it could be read as a law of two states and five states simultaneously depending on how a state was defined. In tracing the vicissitudes of the law over the period 1822 to 1857, I track changes as Comte developed and applied the various modifications he made to his methodologies. He drew attention to the continuity of his thought and when major shifts were brought into the analyses he describes them modestly, downplaying them, even when they are actually very surprising and unexpected. I turn from the stages to the motor which generates them.

I focus attention in particular on the conflict working itself out within the metaphysical state itself and then reassess the general theory in the light of Comte's problems in thinking through this state. What is the metaphysical state? In fact the best way to appreciate Comte's conception is to consider the method by which he presents and analyses it. In almost every discussion of this state in his writing he adopts a form of presentation reserved for it alone. The method of exposition, adopted even in his first essay on the subject of 1820, is in terms of two counter movements presented as two sequences in contrapuntal motion. The first is the series of facts tracing the decline of the medieval unity; it charts the rise of the movement towards free enquiry and conscience, the gradual weakening of the authority and belief systems of Catholicism. The second series charts the rise of science and industry. A feature of the analysis is a consistent effort to compare the different forms of this evolution in Britain and France. The acute manner which the transition took in France was due to the fact that the parliamentary regime was introduced after a more complete destruction of the feudal system than was the case in Britain. The forces of science come to establish an international union on which a new social system will be constructed. In this view, Bonarpartism is not esteemed as a progressive, but is stigmatised as a champion of parasitic neo-feudalism. The next step, he says, is quite different, to complete the installation of the radically new spiritual order based on positive principles.

What I call here the Comtean illusion is the way in which the law of the three states suggests a single sequential chain of cultural forms: theological, metaphysical, positive. It seems that Comte conceived the metaphysical state as a transitional stage in social evolution and one that he had difficulty thinking other than as uniquely riven throughout by internal antagonism. An important thesis which points to the continuity of the sequence is his idea that the emergence of metaphysical phenomena makes it easier to pass between the two extreme states. The question is this: does the transition to the positive stage come through an internal evolutionary development from the metaphysical to the positive polity or does it, by contrast, come from an internal development of the line of the positive movement (science and industry) in a rupture with the metaphysical system? Almost all readers of Comte opt for the first reading. This is the trap of the formula. For example what is the law of the three states? The recent formulation by George Ritzer goes as follows:

> The theory proposes that there are three intellectual stages through which the world has gone throughout its history. According to Comte not only does the world go through this process, but groups, societies, sciences, individuals, and even minds go through the same three stages. The *theological* stage is the first, and it characterised the world prior to 1300. During this period, the major idea system emphasised the belief that supernatural powers, religious figures, modelled after humankind, are at the root of everything. In particular, the social and physical world is seen as produced by God. The second stage is the *metaphysical* stage, which occurred roughly between 1300 and 1800. This era was characterised by the belief that abstract forces like 'nature', rather than personalised gods, explain virtually everything. Finally, in 1800 the world entered the *positivistic* stage, characterised by belief in science. People now tended to give up the search for absolute causes (God or nature) and concentrated instead on observation of the social and physical world in the search for the laws governing them.
>
> (Ritzer, 1996: 14; and cf Ritzer and Goodman, 2004: 84)

The centre piece of the first sociology is this law which Comte presents in the Course as the key organising idea of sociology: all societies necessarily proceed through a stage of theology, then of metaphysics towards a final positive state.

In fact, a number of things are very problematic in this account, which reduces the law to a historical generalisation. This is not Comte's intention, and not what Comte does. It is not Comte's sociology, and certainly if we read what Comte says about methodology and theory it is not what we should expect to find. In fact it would violate everything Comte says about what the new social science should be. The problem here really arises from the fact that almost all the commentators in English rely on Martineau's condensed version of the Course, which is relatively insensitive to theory, and surprisingly perhaps (for Martineau was a novelist) de-dramatises Comte's analyses (which are already highly de-dramatised to conform to scientific requirements). To some extent sociologists have recognised that this is the case and have tried to reflect on what a more subtle understanding of the law might mean. But they have never really travelled very far. The problem is, in Comtean terms, that they have been content to accept the order Comte imposed on his speculations as he came to close down his narratives at the end of each of the phases of his work.

3

The Context and Materials of Sociology

It is important to bear in mind that Comte did not coin the word 'sociology' until 1839. Before that he referred to his social science as a 'social physics' located within the field of 'social physiology'. Nevertheless he claimed to have discovered the basic law of this domain in 1822, a law he baptised as the 'law of the three states'. Every sociologist is aware that the three states are the theological, metaphysical, and the positive. What, however, is the '*law* of the three states'? This is not so easy to answer as it appears and no satisfactory account of it has ever been written.[1]

Comte defined it quite deceptively as a continuous sequential law, a law of succession or filiation, a law of the succession of states. The law itself is thus a dynamics (a study of diachronics, succession) and a 'statics' (a study of synchronics, ensembles). The argument is that human cultures never begin within an already formed scientific knowledge system. They begin, universally, within a framework which is animistic or as he called it, fetishistic, a general framework he classified as 'theological'. Scientific thought becomes predominant and established only after a long evolutionary struggle, passing from the theological, through the metaphysical, to the positive state itself. The law holds that between the theological state and the positive or scientific state of knowledge, there is an intermediary period in which the earlier reign of the spirits or the gods gives way to more abstract entities, such as a more abstract worship of a 'Supreme Being' or other more secularised equivalents, like the abstract forces of natural, or submission to the sovereignty of vague social wills (the will of the people, even the individual 'self'). The third final state, the positive or scientific state, recognises no God or Supreme Being behind the appearances of the world; the world is governed by observable natural laws.

Regarding the thesis of the succession these states can be found in various forms among many thinkers of the seventeenth and eighteenth centuries. In fact the thesis is evidently a synopsis of European history since classical antiquity as it passes from Greek polytheism through Christianity, through the Enlightenment to the notions of democracy and the worship of the 'Supreme Being' in the French Revolution. Comte perceived his own project as confirming this filiation by providing the completion of the three states with his own invention of a social science and its forthcoming applications. He saw his law as explaining the development of human knowledge, and because it was the determining element, the development of all societies – past, future and present.

In effect, therefore Comte's work as a whole is concerned to present, represent, reflect upon, and apply this law and all its implications. Many commentators have discussed this law; at least one (very poor) book is devoted to it (Uta, 1928). Most of these commentaries however are based on and continue serious misunderstandings about it and Comte's own conception of it. The most hostile of critics such as Karl Popper (1961) have mistakenly argued that the very idea of a law of three states is absurd and impossible, and there cannot be any such laws in science. Others have argued that it is a simple evolutionary theory, which because of its teleological form of construction, fails on elementary logical grounds. But whatever the merits of such objections, Comte regarded it as a verifiable law with enormous scope and potential. It could, he thought, at one stroke ground all social theory in relation to a series of empirical facts; it might also be the basis of a genuine unification of all knowledge under the canopy of a science of sciences. Before examining the earliest formulations of the law it is useful here to note two interesting characteristics of this approach.

THE BASIC THREE STATE LAW

It certainly appears in the initial formulations to be a law of culture: knowledge, and methods of producing knowledge are its central objects, and that developments in this order of phenomena are then used to define the stages in progressive social evolution. Thus the question arises directly: what is the connection in fact between the logics of cultural development and wider social progression? Indeed, what is Comte's own idea and definition of 'society'? How are modes of thinking situated and how do they determine the forms of societies? How do steps of intellectual enlightenment pervade and change societies? The second issue concerns the logic of the law itself. Is Comte saying that within the medium of culture itself it is the action of human intelligence, or 'reason' that works out its own path as it passes from religious illusion to scientific knowledge in a classic movement of human enlightenment? Are both order and progress driven by reason and rationalisation?

Comte gives striking answers to these questions, and these answers give the law a much more paradoxical character than might appear. The first is that he by no means holds to a view that society as a whole is permeated by a single mode of thought at any one time. He opens the problem of how different modes of thought co-exist together at any one time, in any one society. But second, and this is more fundamental, the law does, against all appearances, not authorise a conception of progression as a single continuous cultural movement. The law is, as was Comte's work in all its aspects, concerned with revolutions. Living as he did in a crisis ridden post-revolutionary epoch, one that was still resonating with the idea that the recent revolution was not yet completely resolved, he viewed human evolution as, in effect, one vast theatre of revolutionary processes. The 'conservative' part of his project was its explicit concern to play a part in ending – by completing – this process. Before that could be achieved a revolution in social knowledge still had to be accomplished. Sociology was required to form the basis for the construction of a new polity, a 'positive polity' scientifically established.

Comte introduces subtleties into his conception of this project, subtleties which reflect his socio-political values. The first of these is that his law is conceived as one which defines succession, but a succession that is produced as a result of conflict. In fact, each state in the three state sequence is also defined by the predominance of a form of knowledge in each society concerned. As the different forms of knowledge are not neutral towards one another, the internal structure of a society is always in tension. The theological and the positive forms of knowledge, in fact, are inherently incompatible forms; between them, as methods and indeed modes of thinking, there is in his view a permanent and irreconcilable antagonism. This thesis marks out the particularity of Comte's theories for example, which as Kolakowski (1972) has pointed out are clearly Manichean. In this perspective a crucial issue therefore is the conception of the nature and role of the so-called intermediary state; the 'metaphysical state' for this seems to play a kind of mediating role between the basic protagonists. Comte's theory suggests that the development of knowledge can never proceed directly from a theological to a positive state in one revolutionary step – the transition is too abrupt, the abyss too wide. Progression is possible from the theological to the metaphysical states, but that this is not due to the action of an internal logic, simply to human rationality unfolding itself as such. The progression from theological to metaphysical forms is actually the result of the external development of positive reason in the sciences and its complement in the growth of industry and technology, two processes which act from a distance to weaken theology. The real point and location of the break as it were occurs between the metaphysical and scientific states, since metaphysics is really a 'prolongation' of theology rather than being a pure state in itself. The paradoxes of the law are therefore rooted in this conception from the start: although Comte presents a series, the three states are not equivalent to one another nor is there a single uninterrupted progressive movement. The metaphysical state is described from the earliest definitions as a 'hybrid' state, a state without its own unique principle. It exists only because of the combined and conflictual action of the other modes of thought that make it rotate, effect the revolution.

Again, the other two states – those at the beginning and the end of the process – do not 'exist' in the same way either. The theological state has been as the predominant form since the earliest stages of social development, but the positive state has only been achieved in a number of the branches of knowledge in leading Western nations, and not yet in the social domain, and not in any society as a dominant organising principle in a polity. If the law is predictive, it is, in Comte's hands then, not a simple linear evolutionism. There is another subtlety that goes unnoticed in almost all accounts: the order of Comte's analysis is not the expected sequence: state one, state two, leading to state three – as if there was an unfolding essence expanding from a single source. Curiously, but Comte insists on this, the order of analysis is: state one, state three, state two. In other words the way that he approaches the analysis of the metaphysical state is to treat it from the point of view of its position in relation to what he regards as the certain forms of the positive polity (which of course does not yet exist). Another part of the paradox now appears: although his method suggests that the very specificity of science is that it works only in relation to observable phenomena (unlike the methods of theology), his own law of the three states relies entirely on what amounts to a purely imaginary idea of what constitutes the future state from which and toward which the analytic filiation is drawn. But if this third state remains fictional, and he regards it as a well founded scientific fiction, the central object of his analysis must be the directly observable metaphysical state which came into existence with the dissolution of the medieval (feudal-Catholic) polity. He regards the metaphysical state as a long revolutionary transitional phase of Western society, in which the French Revolution is just one important episode. Is it the final episode? When could the final state be said to begin?

This introduction to Comte's sociological concerns gives some indication as to why he was interested, indeed obsessed, with questions of method. For, very far from being a theorist who wanted to document an evolutionary process as it develops throughout history along a single historical dimension, using a naïve empirical method, his elaboration of scientific method was a search for a way to deal with and to analyse a very specific kind of theoretical complexity. Although many of the themes and issues he dealt with were already established in the works of his mentor Saint-Simon, this epistemological complexity is not to be found in his writings. Behind Comte's formulas lies a considerable intellectual effort to pose and legitimise his own theses.

COMTE AND HIS MENTOR SAINT-SIMON

The emergence of Comte's basic sociological framework began under the direct influence of his early mentor Henri Saint-Simon in Paris from 1817–1824. To one of his early essays Comte appended a brief 'Foreword' in which he announced that as a 'pupil of Saint-Simon' he understood their efforts to be working towards the same goal and 'should be viewed as forming one single body of doctrine, tending, by two different routes to the establishment of one and the same political system' (1998: 48). After his break up with Saint-Simon, Comte began to disassociate himself from his influence and his school. Once dismissed, Saint-Simon's influence was then described as an 'unfortunate personal influence' (SSP, IV, appendix II) or denied altogether. It is now clear however that Comte had a very close intellectual relation with Saint-Simon, 'they really loved each other' said Comte's wife (in Pickering, 1993: 230). Almost certainly they lived together (1823–1824). It was Comte who found and probably saved Saint-Simon after a suicide attempt in March 1823. They separated, however, on bad terms. Comte felt betrayed when Saint-Simon not only failed to acknowledge his contributions and originality but put his signature to his pupil's writings. After the break Comte retrospectively over-claimed his own contributions and originality, sometimes to an absurd extent.

From 1817, Comte contributed to a stream of sub-sections of Saint-Simon's publications Comte wrote a very early version of the three state law in 1817 (appearing in the journal *L'Industrie*, vol. 3, 1817) which identified the three states as polytheistic, theological, and positive (Pickering, 1993: 106). He also saw the main line of the genealogy to his own positive politics as traced through Protestantism which he saw as having supported scientific endeavours (Comte, 1970: 95). He also supported the line taken by the 'Doctrinaires' in the Chamber of Deputies that tried to develop parliamentary institutions. Whereas they saw themselves as founding a democratic epoch (see Seidentop, 1979), he saw these institutions as a purely transitional form. Comte in fact wrote the 'Prospectus' to the volume in which he outlined the struggle between the theological system and the anti-theological trends of the eighteenth-century encyclopaedists. He suggested it was now time to begin instead to organise a new morality, a positive morality to replace that based on out-dated theological principles. The new morality would be based on sound foundations, but he noted it 'will not be until the end of the century that the establishment of a truly positive, industrial, and liberal regime will be practicable' (Saint-Simon, 1975: 170).

In his years with Saint-Simon, Comte was hard at work laying the ground for his own version of this vision. Progress was clearly evident in his essay of 1820, later published in his selection from his early works. Although this essay appeared first under the name of Saint-Simon in *L'Organisateur* of April 1820, he republished it in 1854 under his own name as the second of the 'opuscules' a group of six essays, written between 1819 and 1828, which contain the selected essays that form the 'official' version of early Comteanism. The essay crystallises all the preparation that he had accomplished in his attempts from 1815 to come to terms with the restoration of the monarchy in France after the defeat of Napoleon. In its forty pages it is a classic statement of the basic object of social theory. Comte's work is an obsessive fascination with the logic of the three states, understood as a problem of revolutions in knowledge and in society. Perhaps commentators have been too reserved to pose the obvious connections: the trauma of the French Revolution and its Napoleonic false resolutions haunt every page of Comte's vast oeuvre. The reading I present here is based on the idea that Comte finds the revolutionary process everywhere, but in finding everywhere finds it hard to pin down. It is important to note that each science is established in a break with its theological past which, in a revolution signalled by the presence of metaphysical elements, reaches a point of rupture: there is continuity since positivity is established in part by accumulation but also discontinuity because there is displacement.

But there are striking discontinuities of two types. The first is the creative formation of the theoretical organisation of the new science itself – the foundation of the object and domain, a decisive process of discovery which involves the overthrow of metaphysical ideas in this domain. Then second these revolutionary new ideas, which are also organised in a new way, also come into conflict with the ideas and principles which rule in any society dominated by theological or metaphysical powers. He is always on the look out for the ways these powers block scientific development or are engaged in a struggle with it. Comte therefore has a conception of antagonism, a term he introduced into the social sciences and which he analysed in a number of different modes. Between theological and positive forms of thought there is he argued an inevitable opposition: but the antagonism between them only becomes acute at certain points of social development. This occurs when certain sciences are in the process of formation, and their formation involves a direct assault on elements central to theological power, and when the whole body of the sciences begins to become a threat to the systematic power of the theological state. Thus it is a travesty in a sense to present Comte's analysis of the sciences as a simple history of ideas. It is in fact an account of the series of revolutions in human theoretical culture that led him to confront the general crisis of eighteenth- and nineteenth-century European societies. The law of the three states is the equivalent in Comte's thought to the revolutionary dialectic in Marx: it is a logic of rupture. In this reading, therefore, I avoid all temptations to see in this logic any parallel with a series of natural states. Instead it was proposed in order to think about the logic of revolutionary transitions, or of complex developmental processes in which conflicts and tensions are produced, and in which outcomes are sometimes blocked or diverted or deferred. The investigation here is then an attempt to discover the nature of this logic and how it came to be the object of a sociological law.

The law of the three states was discovered once but was rediscovered and developed in many different directions for varying purposes. Comte himself was aware that he presented the law in different ways, or as he said it appeared under 'different aspects' between 1822 and his death in 1857. I want to begin by discussing the first set of presentations in his works – the first in the early opuscules and the works up till 1844. It was perhaps characteristic that there was a long build up in Comte's writings from the early sketches and preliminary outlines in 1817 to the point at which Comte decided on the form of the law in 1822 (see Pickering, 1993: 199ff.). And when these so-called 'opuscules' were reprinted as an appendix to the System (volume IV) in 1854, he claimed that they demonstrated the consistency between the early ambitions and the completion of the project in the later works. However, as I shall show, there is a considerable shift in the expositions of the law in the first cycle to those in the second.

THE (RAW) MATERIALS FOR A SOCIOLOGY

This is not the place to discuss how Comte arrived at the ideas in his 1820 essay. What is significant here is that they are presented without any elaborate philosophical or methodological scaffolding. In this sense the essay (included in Comte, 1998) is raw Comteanism, or more accurately Comteanism in its original, 'Saint-Simonian' form. Saint-Simon was fifty-nine when he published this essay under his own name. Comte, the actual author, was twenty-two. If the essay could be read legitimately as a logical development out of Saint-Simon's own considerable output, this is because most of the vision and terminology of the essay had been established in the years before 1820, in fact even before 1815, the year in which Saint-Simon proposed an Anglo-French 'spiritual power' made up of 'savants' and 'industriels' to rule Europe after the defeat of Napoleon at Waterloo. Comte's own formulations were couched in a different, more coherent and empirically specific language. His general conception was that European history could be read as a long transition, moving from a military-theological feudal system to a system based on industry and science.

The first system was in terminal decline. The second system was approaching the point of full completion. Comte's essay is again organised in his characteristic manner: he presents (1998: 10–20) a 'series' of facts detailing the process of decline of the first system. A second 'series' details the rise to ascendancy of the new one (1998: 20–42). Comte conceives the industrial-scientific system as establishing itself externally to and in direct competition with the feudal-theocratic order. In fact the analysis is presented very much as a competition between articulated couples in which the feudal couple (theological and military) is replaced by the modern couple (scientific and industrial). As couples, their component elements rise or fall together. The key facts relating to the new system are the introduction of the sciences into Europe in the Middle Ages from Arab cultures – and this is conceived as another fundamental externality, and what Comte calls the 'enfranchisement of the communes', the transition from serfdom and feudal bondage to independence (see Clauzade, 1996). The development of industrial property is for Comte again a process he conceives as occurring outside of and independently from the logic of feudal military culture. Although the 'temporal' power remained in the hands of a military elite, 'industrial capacity could develop, progress and expand, and nations could organise themselves in all their parts on an industrial basis …' (1998: 7).

Throughout his essay, Comte notes in an important theoretical subtlety that whereas the old system was based on two 'powers' (theological and military) the new system is based on 'capacities', because he wants to argue that there is here a fundamental shift in the forms of governmentality itself, away from the dictatorship of individuals to the administration of laws. The division and separation of the spiritual from the temporal power in the medieval period makes it possible for the sciences to engage with theory in a space of its own, independent to a high degree of political power. The separation will not only continue to exist, but it will be the major feature of the future order. It seems essential in considering his ideas in this early essay not to reduce its logic to a one dimensional account of the transition from feudalism to industrialism. Very specifically in this argument the transition is understood to proceed from agrarian to industrial society, not from military to industrial (a term which is defined to include crafts and manufacture); this is not an evolution but a displacement. Feudalism can make come-backs; Napoleon represents for example the desire to return to the past, militarism and theocracy (1998: 37).

These ideas can be seen to be a particular variation on Saint-Simonian themes, themes which were to be the basis of very different elaborations and variations after Saint-Simon's death in 1825 by the Saint-Simonian school led by Bazard and Enfantin. This school crystallised Saint-Simon's ideas into the 'doctrine' of 1829 with the first proto-Marxist theory of exploitation of man by man and its curious religious organisation and rituals (Cunliffe and Reeve, 1996). In 1820 Comte did not elaborate a doctrine of exploitation but he did lay out the ground referring critically to parasites, 'schemers and men of ambition', and to 'the idle and parasitic class' (1998: 37), which he identifies as the remnants of the old feudalism. This is not the only phenomenon linked to the old order. It is important to note that in this early essay he introduces an account – parallel to that being elaborated by the 'Doctrinaires' – of the different ways especially concerning the relation of kings to aristocracies in which the transition has taken place in Britain as compared with France which allows him to locate political institutions in a social process. In Britain the feudal powers formed an alliance with the 'commons' against royalty (1998: 11). The analysis of the 'House of Commons' suggests that this is not linked in any essential way to the new system, but is an institution initially dependent on the forces of its original milieu. It has played ambivalent roles, often manipulated by the powers of the old system to their advantage. The royal power in France developed at the expense of the feudal aristocracy, but from Louis XIV it abandoned its strategic alliance with the 'communes', and from that moment the decline of the old system entered its terminal phase. If the revolution in France was a 'wrong turning' in the transition the introduction of English constitutional forms put it back on track by establishing in a new conjuncture the true 'means of transition' – the chamber representing public opinion – and only this, he says, will permit the peaceful completion of the process of the new system, for in the French case parliamentary democracy is only introduced after 'the modification of the old system was far greater than in England' (1998: 31).

THESE HISTORICAL RAW MATERIALS PLACED IN THE FRAME OF A SCIENTIFIC LAW

If we look now at the next early essay or opuscule, the third, called 'Plan of the Scientific Work Necessary for the Reorganisation of Society' which Comte regarded as the fundamental one, there is a very basic alteration in the mode of presentation. From now on Comte applies the full panoply of his own new methodology, and with it there come a number of theoretical reconsiderations. If the Foreword to the second expanded version of this paper published in 1824 acknowledges Saint-Simon and says that their works form 'one single body of doctrine' (1998: 48) it is interesting, nonetheless, to look at the differences between the text of 1820 and those of 1822–1824 to examine the effects of introducing the three state law itself and its new way of conceptualising and organising the historical material already in place in 1820.

It is clear that the first enunciation of the law of the three states was embedded in an argument in favour of a new attitude to political and social affairs. From now on, he argued, there was an urgent need for observation to rule imagination in political thought, and there should be an acceptance that social development is a determined process: first, the degree of social organisation is determined by the level civilisation (science, art, industry), and second, the level of civilisation is determined by forces that are as yet undiscovered. From these propositions a number of conclusions follow: the process itself is a 'social fact', is law-governed, occuring outside of individuals themselves. It is in principle an historical inevitability though such processes may be open to a degree of modification by social action. Rather contradicting what he had said about Napoleon I, he said social developments are not caused by individual action and so individuals should not take praise or blame for them. Even if earlier attempts to understand these processes (Montesquieu, Condorcet) were failures, it is time to begin again, for it is clear that the association of scientists and industrialists represents the emergence of new temporal and spiritual powers; and only through their intervention can 'long and terrible convulsions' be averted. Only advanced 'scientific prevision can avert or mitigate violent revolutions' (1974a: 148).

Comte's evocation of an avoidable apocalypse leads to the plea for new ways of assessing with precision the 'real tendency of civilisation' (1974a: 150). Surprisingly, in complete contradiction to the emphasis on the primacy on observation, he argues that a simple and direct observation of the current state cannot produce knowledge of a developmental tendency. The only way to establish the existence of a real tendency is to be able to establish the fixed point between two terms, and a verification is established by discovery of a third in relation to them. It is essential he adds to be able to distinguish between the chronological order and the terms of a philosophical order: the latter is effective only through scientific prevision, in the order: past, future, present. Thus observation, the basis of the new spirit, does not follow the order of empirical chronology (p. 153). The discovery of new laws will install relative in place of arbitrary or absolute thought, and will enable disputes to be resolved by reference to scientific law, so that 'government by measures replaces government by men' (p. 154). Society will reorganise itself by taking production as 'its only and constant aim' (pp.162–3). The methods for the study of this law are then outlined: the essential order is that the first studies should 'aim at establishing the general progress of mankind, putting aside the various causes that may modify the rate ...' and only then should other investigations be undertaken to estimate the 'influence of their modifying elements' (p. 177).

This remarkable essay of 1822 contains then the first significant statement of the three state law, in both the intellectual and the social domain. The necessity for understanding human progress is to avoid the perils of more convulsions and to pass from the regime transition, to the final system. In an important concluding statement he says: 'In our day three different Systems coexist in the heart of society: the theologico-feudal system, the scientific-industrial system, and lastly the hybrid and transitional system of metaphysicians and lawyers' (1974a: 152). In the discussion of this co-existence, he identifies the doctrines of the sovereignty of people as the metaphysical equivalent of the theological doctrine of the divine right of kings. The doctrine of complete liberty of conscience is identified as effective only in the period of the critique of theology, but it ceases to be progressive 'and loses all value when conceived as a basis for the great social reorganisation reserved for our epoch … (when) it constitutes an obstacle' indeed if this 'error could last, the reorganisation of society would be forever impossible' (pp. 115–16). The law is not absolute.

The introduction of the law of the three states as an organising frame has a number of consequences for Comte's initial outline. It lengthened the trajectory of the historical sequence to include what Comte considered the earliest states: Egypt at the beginning stretching to include what he considered would be the future spiritual power at the end. It re-baptised the states along the route by introducing the concept of the 'metaphysical' state as an intermediary, and by subdividing the theological stage. It introduced a new sequence of the increasing division of labour in the intellectual sphere (incidentally the final state now included a partnership of scientists, engineers and what he calls '*industriels*'). There was a new characterisation within the metaphysical state itself, with a new couple: lawyers and philosophers as the leading strata. There was a characterisation of the problems of this new state arising from the absence of a spiritual power: mental, economic and social anarchy. There was new detail in the comparative analysis of the different ways in which the transition was being accomplished (France on the one hand, and Britain on the other). The working out of the development of the sciences became increasingly sophisticated and linked to a new genealogy of the elements of which were evolving towards the positive polity. The basic and fundamental antagonism between science and religion was also much more clearly delineated.

It seems evident from reading these two essays that Comte's main concern is the logic of the growth of the sciences and how this growth has consequences for other forms of knowledge and for the articulation of the elements within societies as wholes. It would be wrong to say that there is an appeal to some overriding metaphysical force such as Reason, or that Comte is interested to follow a single line of rationalisation through different societies. The specific features of the 'modern crisis' that he identifies – bureaucracy, egoism, materialism – arise out of imbalances and incomplete development of institutions. After 1820 his interest in the 'enfranchisement of the communes' is put to one side, and the analysis becomes focused on the transition to the new spiritual power, on the relations of *savants* to its organisation of knowledge.

Some of the central elements of Comte's social theory emerge at this point. He argues that the principle of the sovereignty of the people goes hand in hand with the principle of unlimited freedom of individual conscience. 'In proclaiming the sovereignty of each individual mind, this principle in fact tends essentially to prevent the uniform establishment of any system of general ideas; yet without them there can be no society'. Liberty of criticism is rightly given full range against a system of beliefs which are in decline in order 'to hasten their fall' (1998: 55). The two principles, the two claims to sovereignty, must come to an end with the construction of the new society for 'both of them were born to destroy, they are equally incapable of constructing' (1998: 56). When a new system comes into existence, its intellectual basis, the results of science, is to be found in a new principle of trust and then the critical epoch is over.

4

The Intimations of Social Science and a New Politics

In fact it is not until the 'opuscule' of November 1825, 'Philosophical Considerations on the Sciences and Savants', which opens dramatically with a third full statement of the law, that he explores some of its implications, and even here he left his arguments at a fairly elementary level of elaboration. In 1825 (November–December) he presented his law as follows:

> Man began by conceiving phenomena of all kinds as due to the direct and continuous influence of supernatural agents; he next considered them as produced by different abstract forces residing in matter, but distinct and heterogeneous; finally, he limited himself to considering them as subject to a certain number of invariable natural laws.
>
> (1998: 145)

The essay, however is really an attempt to pose another type of question: what will be the new organisational form of the intellectuals (the 'savants') themselves? The first part of the discussion proposes the law as one of cognitive development, and Comte introduces the series: fetishism, polytheism, monotheism, as the principal theological sub-phases followed by the metaphysical and positive states. He argues that it is important to understand why this sequence exists: it is he says because the basic antagonism between the theological and the positive is too radical and 'heterogeneous' to 'allow our intelligence [to pass] from one to the other without intermediate steps' (1998: 187). The difference between the theological and the positive method is at base an epistemological one:

> Theological philosophy, placing itself at the prime source of all phenomena, is essentially occupied in unfolding their efficient causes, while positive philosophy – laying aside all search after causes, as being inaccessible to the human mind – is exclusively occupied in discovering laws, that is to say, the constant relations of similitude and succession which subsist between facts … Between these two points of view is naturally interposed the metaphysical, which regards each phenomenon as the product of an abstract force peculiar to itself.
>
> (1998:187–8)

Only with the completion of the series of sciences with a social science will the remedy for mental and moral anarchy be found.

THE NATURE OF THE THREE STATE LAW

From the beginning of his discussions of the law and the main sequence of sub-states he continually emphasised that it was not to be conceived as a number of historical blocks strung out in homogeneous time. He appealed to the writings of Adam Smith to note that 'man was never completely theologian. There were always some phenomena simple enough and regular enough for him to regard them, even from the outset, as subject to natural laws' (1998: 147). And his conception even drew attention to the fact that since the sciences were not formed simultaneously, 'there must have been periods, longer or shorter, during which the human mind employed the three methods at once, each for a certain order of ideas' (1998: 163). He admitted at this point that attempts to verify the law encounter their most significant difficulties precisely because of the co-existence of methodologies – 'the fact of this mixed state is, moreover, the only serious objection that has been made, to my knowledge, against this fundamental law' (1998: 163).

The interpretation of this sequence establishes a general theory of culture. In each culture there is always a certain definite combination of methodical observation of the world and forms of theoretical reasoning. Indeed in every culture the observation of the world is always dependent on theory: 'Man is by his nature incapable not only of comparing facts and deducing some consequences from them, but even simply of observing them carefully, and remembering them reliably, if he does not immediately connect them with some explanation' (1998: 149). Comte is always alert to the possible accusation that he might be interpreted as suggesting the positive sciences are merely techniques of collecting, accumulating and storing facts. Curiously in one sense he goes further in trying to limit their scope: sciences are not, he says, even interested in the ultimate 'mode of production' of the phenomena they study. They are concerned only with establishing laws and explaining them (and this activity however has to have recourse to theory).

His theory of knowledge then is not restricted to the internal logic of the branches of knowledge themselves; his historical epistemology is embedded in social history. 'These two elements', theoretical culture and society, 'although distinct from one another, are not independent' he said. 'On the contrary, they exert on one another an influence that is continuous and indispensable to both … the nature and extent of social relations determine in every age the character and the pace of our spiritual progress, and vice versa' (1998: 151). Knowledge progresses when there is a special stratum of intellectuals devoted to spiritual affairs. A fundamental division of social labour underpins the development of the sciences. This general theory is certainly a 'conflict theory'. If there is an antagonism in principle between theological and positive methods, referring constantly to the 'radical heterogeneity of theology and physics' (1998: 178) his conception suggests that metaphysical conceptions are effectively brought into existence by the struggle between the two methods, as a secularised continuation of theological modes of thought. They are, he repeats, to be considered as 'means of transition' (1998: 153) from one state to another.

The theory of the evolution of the sciences has by 1825 also been made more sophisticated and established itself in this order: astronomy, physics, chemistry, and physiology (a category which includes the life sciences, 'individual physiology' and the social sciences). He says to avoid any confusion … 'I understand by social physics the science whose distinctive object is the study of social phenomena' (1998: 159). The attitude adopted in such a study is to consider:

> social facts, not as objects to be admired or criticized, it is solely concerned with establishing their mutual relations and grasping the influence exercised by each of them on the overall pattern of human development. In its relations to practice it removes any absolute idea of good or evil from the different institutions and regards them consistently as relative to the particular state of society, and variable with it.
>
> (1998: 159)

The new politics is thus conceived as being quite different from the old absolutism, and Comte does not hold back from embracing a relativist position. Indeed he sees the new science as coming into existence only on the basis of this relativism. The new science creates the possibility of establishing a new kind of politics:

> The purpose of such a science is to provide the positive point of departure for the work of the statesman, which thus no longer has any other real object than to discover and institute the practical forms corresponding to the these fundamental data, in order to avoid or at least soften as much as possible the crises – more or less serious – which spontaneous development brings about when it is not foreseen. In short, in this order of phenomena as in any other, science leads to foresight, and foresight allows us to regulate action.
>
> (1998: 160)

THE 'SPIRITUAL' POWER AND A NEW KIND OF INTELLECTUAL HEGEMONY

A sketch of this series is further developed in the fifth 'opuscule', 'Considerations on the Spiritual Power' written when Comte was twenty-eight (March, 1826), in an account of the new spiritual power which begins to identify its functions:

a the government of opinion and maintenance of the principles governing social relations;
b education, which would include teaching the modern encyclopaedia, but it would also include representing social principles in active life;
c the new learned corporation would have a consultative role in politics;
d it would arbitrate on disputes across the whole of Europe;
e it would provide for government the intellectual means of regulating the division of labour.

In the pure case, such a corporation would exercise a harmonising and pacifying influence. It should aim to be the equivalent of such institutions in the ancient and medieval world where it was clear that what was governed by force was only that portion of government that could not be regulated by authoritative opinion (1998: 213). Such a formulation harked back to Comte's first opuscule which distinguished clearly between the sphere of public opinion which should represent to authority its desires, and the sphere of competent government which should take up and act to fulfil those desires. In the absence of such a power, the problem of order becomes acute (and Comte here refers to

Hobbes directly (1998: 217)). Until such a general European authority is in place, its 'order will be constantly on the point of being compromised' (1998: 224–5). In relation to specific problems such as the relation of employers to labour, and the precise nature of social stratification, it is, he says, only such a new spiritual power which can provide the new morality and the means of rational social classification to overcome the evident current social and economic anarchy. Comte develops then, not a theory of economic exploitation, but a theory of the injustice of social mis-classification: from each according to his capacity to each according to his contribution (1974b: 104). Marxists generally have not recognised the role Comte played in the construction of socialist principles in his Saint-Simonian period).

SOCIAL PATHOLOGY

Comte's work in 1820 concerned the transition from European feudalism to a new Europe based on science and industry. After the introduction of the framework of the three state law another logic is added, one that rounds out as a complement of the purely intellectual dynamic a series of observations and ideas about the 'social systems' implied by it. Thus the theory becomes much more explicit about the 'system' of mediaeval Catholicism, which tends to become an ideal type, its structure made into something of a model 'normal state' (as opposed to the 'exceptional' metaphysical state). The last, the sixth, 'opuscule' in a way addresses this issue from a new point of view. It was written in 1828, after he returned to intellectual work from his personal breakdown, as a review of the concept of pathology developed by Broussais. Broussais' revolution was to argue that abnormal phenomena are extreme phenomena, phenomena pushed beyond certain limits, not phenomena of an altogether different order of nature. Thus the field of the life sciences is at a stroke unified epistemologically. What was once held to be a domain of two fundamentally different kinds of phenomena, the study of each requiring its own methodology, is now to be treated as variations in the intensities of phenomena. The methodological reflection shifts to take up the problem of identifying the proper limits of variation beyond which life is no longer normal (a basic theme of the life sciences in Comte's period, see Nye, 1998: 65).

Can one of the states in the law of the three states ever be said to be abnormal or pathological? Is the metaphysical state such a state? In the early essays Comte refers to the metaphysical state as 'hybrid', a state which does not rest on its own unique principle. By focusing attention on the 'normal' states (one historical, one virtual), Comte's interest in the 'metaphysical' state, though central, is from now on actually somewhat disguised. There are two linked ambiguities. One is the ambiguous and as yet undefined specific character of the future state. The other is the status of the second state. Are the features of anarchy, corruption, egoism, bureaucracy, pathologies or normal characteristics of this state? Indeed, the excesses of the French Revolution itself, were these pathologies of revolution or was the revolution itself a pathological event of the transition period?

If we turn to the revolution for a moment, it is clear that in these essays and Comte was consistent in his view that having broken the state power at the highest level the progressive movement was entering the beginning of the final phase of the transition to the new polity. Yet the revolution had taken a wrong path and, with Napoleon, had been set on a regressive course to establish retrograde militaristic feudalism. The question arises: what precisely went wrong with the course of modernity?

Comte's many comparisons between France and Britain, which parallel those elaborated by the liberal 'Doctrinaires' (Seidentop, 1979) had the purpose of arguing that France was in a better position than Britain to forge the development of the final state. In Britain the institutions of the 'commons' have been used by the aristocracy to secure its own position of dominance. In France these institutions could be free from the limitations put on them in the British case. In France the opposition to the spread of Protestantism meant that there was a greater likelihood that a real corporation, on the model of a priesthood, could be constructed that would establish a new spiritual power. But from his remarks on the role of public opinion, it is clear that Comte thought the 'people' would remain 'passive' in any further transition: they would be consulted but they would not play an active role. His conception is one that divides social action between intention, council and execution. And here he is consistent. In the transition it is the ruling elites that count. Even here, in such a transition, it is of secondary importance which elites actually come to power, for in the long run the logic of the process is sure to produce the same outcome. Napoleon was a transitory figure, running against the main stream. There are mainstream, long term processes, and temporary aberrations, oscillations, or deviations from the main path. The process is never in fact democratically decided, for intellectual elites that provide the organ of counsel can be catapulted into power and influence according to the inclination of the temporal power itself (Napoleon's promotion of Benjamin Constant, or for example the rise to influence of Victor Cousin in the Restoration period).

These issues raise the question of Comte's own strategic thinking. How were the final steps in the transition to be accomplished? At this early stage it does not appear that he had in mind a return to organised religion as the normal form in which the future state would be realised. He is, in these early essays, scathing in respect to absurdities of religious fantasies (1974a: 154). After he had broken with Saint-Simon in 1824, Saint-Simon certainly turned to religion, as his 'Nouveau Christianisme' of 1825 shows. This was quickly taken up by new disciples who took to the 'Religion of Saint-Simon' enthusiastically, leaving Comte on one side (out of the scene for many months in any case with a nervous breakdown). Comte claimed the doctrine of the new religion could not be found in Saint-Simon's writings and that the new cult resembled merely a fetishistic and pathological parody of Catholicism. As with religions that exercise control over what counts as truth Comte – although he did not even belong to it – was soon to be excommunicated in principle from the religion.

It seems, then, that at this time Comte did not think the future polity entailed the birth of a religious cult; indeed he was extremely hostile to the idea. He ridiculed de Maistre's notion of a return to supernatural Christianity. He then, unlike 1817, ridiculed all suggestions that there could be an internal evolution of a priestly caste into a scientific one, drawing the conclusion that the failure of the Jesuits to develop itself into a scientifically competent corporation proved that no priesthood would be capable of such a transformation. Such failures revealed that these forms would be abnormal ones in the new conditions. His view was that there was a need for a new corporation, a college, of teachers and researchers established as scientists (savants) founded on the new encyclopaedic order of scientific knowledge. He tried to get posts in higher educational institutions to develop these ideas, but he failed. However, as he realised, scientists themselves tended to be specialists not generalists, and that such an emphasis on specialism actually contributed to the intellectual anarchy he was trying to oppose. Here he was optimistic. He saw himself as a new kind of generalist, able to work in all the main branches of scientific knowledge and especially in the new field of 'social physics' within 'social physiology' a field destined to play a leading role in harmonising all knowledge. The new type of intellectual was to play the role of forming knowledge into a unified system, of connecting all the elements of the new system together, of developing them into a position where it could play a leading moral role. The theory of the system of the sciences was therefore to be completed with a theory of the social system of scientists themselves, with the generalists at the top of the hierarchy. This hierarchy was not a simple linear rank order but a system in which each position marked the way in which the sciences themselves were different from each other in the encyclopaedia. Even this emerging system revealed from the start the signs of pathological mal-formation.[1] If Weber could later assert that methodology is 'no more the precondition of fruitful intellectual work than the knowledge of anatomy is the precondition for 'correct walking' (in Bryant, 1985: 78), Comte radically argues that this emerging society cannot be born and cannot function without its own scientific self-consciousness.

THE FINAL WRITINGS OF THE EARLY PERIOD

Comte was a teacher. He taught privately, and for a time in a boarding school. He examined for the Ecole Polytechnique, and also gave lecture courses, his own initiative, to large public audiences on astronomy. He is however, most famous for his *Course in Positive Philosophy*, which he started to present to an impressive audience in the beginning of 1826. He was forced to interrupt the course soon after it commenced when he succumbed to an acute personal breakdown which lasted from April 1826 to the beginning of 1827. Although the first volume of the Course itself was published in 1830, the introductory lectures were published in December 1829 – the idea was to publish the lectures as they were written in the *Revue Encyclopédique* and then bind them together when he had finished a set of eighteen. The first volume which is dated July 1830 thus contains two introductory lectures, and sixteen lectures on mathematics. The next volume, on astronomy, however, did not appear until 1834. The second group of writings which focus on social theory and analysis in the later part of the Course should really be considered to begin a new period of thinking at the end of the 1830s (with lectures 46–60 which I discuss later). There was a hiatus. Mary Pickering noted that 'The most salient fact of Comte's life in the early 1830s was that he apparently did not devote any attention at all' to the Course. In effect the two introductory lectures published in November and December 1829 effectively sum up the ideas of the opuscules and should be grouped with them, along with the short Author's Preface ('Advertissement de l'Auteur') which was written in December 1829 to introduce the Course.

In the first two lectures of the Course, published in 1829 but probably written much earlier, he presents the law of the three states following almost word for word his early formulaic pronouncements, with none of the subtleties he had introduced in the other 'opuscules'. And in his Author's Preface to the Course, he notes carefully why the work is called a course in philosophy. He notes that in fact it was with 'regret' that he 'was obliged to adopt (philosophy), for want of another term. He did not chose the expression philosophy of the sciences, natural philosophy, philosophy of the positive sciences, or similar expression, because the object of analysis is what he calls 'the generalities of the different sciences, conceived as submitting to a single method and as forming different parts of a general plan of research' (1975: I, vi). In the first lecture he repeats that the work is called *Course in Positive Philosophy*, and 'not by accident'. He continues, 'It is a question here to consider each of the fundamental sciences in their relations with the system of the sciences as a whole, and in relation to the spirit which characterises it, that is to say under the double relation of its essential methods and its principal results' (1975: I, 30).

The project of the lecture course could not have been more ambitious: it was nothing less than to sum up, complete and organise the system of the sciences conceived as having its own traditions, trajectory and destination quite independently from religion. The place of 'social physics' in the course is pivotal. This raises an obvious question: is Comte writing a text of foundational social science, or is he writing a text on the philosophy of the new social science in the positive system of the sciences? He states the objective quite clearly: the 'special' goal of the course is in fact to write the founding text of a new social science, 'a course in social physics'; the 'second' more general objective is to establish the new system of the sciences as a universal system capable of replacing theology and metaphysics, 'a course in positive philosophy' (1975: I, 29). His programme was maximal: both to found a new science and to found a new of philosophy. He is certainly acutely aware the problems he is facing in tacking two orders of analysis, but in a sense he claims that most of the work in found social science has already been successfully begun with his own work on the law of the three states, and that given his reflections on scientific method, the more satisfactory working out of the law would not create insuperable difficulties. The first half of the Course (volumes I–III, lectures 1–45), are in the new philosophical mode and aimed at organising the sciences. The second half of the Course, (volumes IV–VI, lectures 46–57), sets the scene for the foundation of a new science (the word sociology first appears in print in lecture 47). The last three lectures (58, 59 and 60) are Comte's reflections on positive methods as a whole and integrates the sociology into the positive hierarchy.

The law that appears in the first pages of the Course in 1830 is the formula that appears in the third 'opuscule' (of 1822, see 1998: 81). 'Each branch of our knowledge passes successively through three different theoretical states: the theological or fictive; the metaphysical or abstract; the scientific, or positive' (1975: I, 21). Each of the three methods has a unique character and are radically opposed to one another; they are 'mutually exclusive' (p. 21). The very first explanations of the external world are made via a recourse to 'supernatural agents' whose arbitrary actions explain everything; in the second, the supernatural agents are replaced by 'abstract forces, veritable entities (personified abstractions) inherent in the diverse beings of the world, and conceived as capable of engendering by themselves all observed phenomena; the explanation consists in assigning for each observed phenomenon one of the corresponding abstractions' (p. 21).

In fact this exposition of the law in 1829 is not as complex as the discussion in the 'opuscules' of 1824 and 1825. The presentation emphasises linearity, continuity, and the steps along a single progressive pathway to the completion of the scientific series. He gives in the first lecture a theoretical justification of the law and in particular the idea that the metaphysical state is an 'intermediate system of conceptions, with a hybrid character (d'un caractère bâtard) necessary to render the transition possible'. Why is this? Simply because 'theology and physics are so profoundly incompatible, (and) their concepts have a character so radically opposed' to one another (p. 24). At the end of the first lecture Comte introduces a striking conclusion. In the last analysis, he says, it is because the three methods are still being employed without any coherence, that social reorganisation is made impossible. Comte closes off his first period of discussion of the law of the three states by claiming that it is the rise of positive philosophy itself makes social reorganisation possible, the transition to the higher society, 'by completing the vast intellectual operation begun by Bacon, Descartes and Galileo … the revolutionary crisis which torments the civilized peoples will come to an end' (p. 39).

The law now has reached a stable form. Comte outlines a genealogy which traces the effect of the general law through Egypt, Greece, Rome, the Catholic Middle Ages, and the rise of modern science, and is rooted in this empirical series. The discussion focuses on the fusion of the spiritual and temporal powers in antiquity and their clear separation in the middle ages. Modern opinion (such as that of Hobbes (1946: 79) for example) wrongly concludes that either the spiritual power should be subordinated to the temporal or should not exist independently of it. The evident problem in Comte's argument is that he wants to argue that there is a specific genealogy of 'savants' who will organise the new spiritual power. But what is the role of the metaphysicians in this series? Curiously but logically at this point in Comte's thinking the beginnings of the emergence of metaphysical phenomena is pushed back into antiquity. In a discussion of the evolution of liberty of expression, the sovereignty of the people, and social equality, or what he calls the 'critical doctrine', over the last three centuries, he argues that what emerges is 'the strange phenomenon, inexplicable to anyone who has not followed its historical development: political and moral disorder elevated into a system and presented as an ideal'(1974a: 217). Avoiding any direct analysis of the critical doctrines and indeed of the metaphysicians in the genealogy, he makes the general point that whenever there is a passage from one regime to another there arises a period of 'moral anarchy'. And:

> this anarchical character, of necessity, developed itself, in the highest degree, during the period of the disorganization of the Catholic and Feudal system, since what the revolution then demanded was the greatest change in the whole course of human history, the direct transition from the theological and military to the positive and industrial state, compared with which all previous revolutions were simple modifications. (p. 216)

The concept of the metaphysical state is here transformed into a period of revolutionary anarchy lasting several centuries.

THE EARLY WRITINGS AS A WHOLE

We can now examine the essays after 1820 as a whole to analyse in more detail what happened when Comte introduced the apparatus of the positive method and the law of the three states into his materials. Clearly the most important development is the introduction of the key idea of the metaphysical state, and more generally what he calls the 'spirit of the metaphysical stage' as the designation of the transitional state between the other two states (1998: 164–5). More specifically he begins to flesh out examples and now identifies as metaphysical, Aristotle's ideas on celestial and terrestrial physics, the Scholastic doctrines of the Middle Ages, and Rousseau's notions of the social contract and the sovereignty of the people (1998: 164–5). Behind these examples is a far more elaborate justification for the concept of metaphysics which is only fully presented some years later.

An important element in Comte's emerging framework is the detailed working out of the genealogy of the new position. He identifies Montesquieu, Hume, Smith and Ferguson, Kant and Herder, and importantly, de Maistre (1998: 166), as the key precursors. A completely new order of knowledge is in the process of being established he proclaims, and the construction of a new encyclopaedia will be undertaken. This will be different from all previous ones, since it will now come into existence after 'theology and metaphysics have been chased from their last refuge' (1998: 167). In contrast to the encyclopaedia of the eighteenth century, this one will be positive, homogeneous and universal, the true completion of the project outlined by Bacon and Galileo.

The range and scope of his analysis was broadened from that of 1820 where it focused on the transition from the Catholic-Feudal to the Scientific-Industrial system. After the first, fetishist period comes the theological period proper, one marked by the emergence of the 'general and absolute preponderance of a learned caste, organised under the influence of theological philosophy'. Comte gives an idea of the scope of his analysis which now includes ancient Egypt, Chaldea, Hindustan, Tibet, China, Japan, Peru, and Mexico. In the ancient world, the typical, or model intellectual (savant), such as Moses, would combine all the available kinds of knowledge in his philosophy and religious outlook (1998: 171).With the Ancient Greeks there was the opening up of a new major division of labour between a purely speculative body of thinkers concerned with speculative issues, and other bodies concerned with practical, and military affairs. In the former there were the beginnings also of a division of interest between philosophy and the arts on the one hand and the theological work of a purely priestly corporation (1998: 175). At this point he makes a characteristic observation: even in the case of Greece the introduction of scientific pursuits were stimulated from outside, externally (1998: 175). When the sciences become established alongside polytheism in Greece there also emerges an 'abstract metaphysical character which then begins to appear clearly in the intellectual system'. There then follows a division in the intellectual realm itself between those who specialise in natural science (like Aristotle), and those who specialise more and more in metaphysical philosophical issues (like Plato). The development of the sciences is then continued by non-Platonist thinkers. And the decline of scientific creativity occurred long before the fall of Rome (1998: 179). In the Middle Ages science is re-introduced again externally from the Arab cultures (where science was carried alongside but still at a distance from Islam).

With the growth of science and industry there is a marked politicisation of the sciences. The radical changes in the authority of the spiritual power, and the rise and consolidation of the temporal power of kings and national states, led to the opening of a new void which is characteristic of modern cultures. Comte characterises this as a new 'mental anarchy', a marked absence of public morality, the rise of egoism and materialistic values, and in the state unparalleled centralisation, bureaucratisation and corruption (1998: 196–9). His solution is to propose to try to envision and to construct a new spiritual power, one which could achieve a unity and universality equal to the medieval papacy. It cannot, he says, simply reproduce the theological system of medieval Catholicism, as was being argued by the ultras in the Chamber of Deputies (Seidentop, 1979: 153–75); this has lost all legitimacy. It is clear that a new version of such a power would not necessarily be weaker or less extensive in its range of authority, but rather the reverse: the 'intervention of the spiritual power must be more explicit and more complete' than in the Middle Ages he argued (1998: 204).

Having outlined the course of social development and identified the main forms of conflict within it, Comte began to think about a new kind of politics. He found, as we have seen in this chapter, in the concept of pathology a way in which to get beyond not only the religious categories of good and evil, but also the more metaphysical categories elaborated by the metaphysicians in their doctrines of freedom, liberalism, democracy, human justice and rights. It was a way to develop the ideas he had expressed on overcoming arbitrary political rule and his views on the new role of statesmen as establishing and maintaining the course of history discovered by science.

5

Comte's Heretical Report on Knowledge

The period of the 1840s was one in which the first epistemological wars over the social sciences in the modern sense were to be fought. Nietzsche was certainly wrong to think Comte was a 'great honest Frenchman beside whom, as embracer and conqueror of the strict sciences, the Germans and English of this century can place no rival' (Nietzsche [1881], 1982: 215), since Peirce (1982: 205–23) at Harvard was far nearer the truth in reporting in 1865 the main protagonists were clearly Comte, Mill, and Whewell. In 1866 Marx wrote to Engels that he was reading this 'shit-positivism' because it was so in vogue (Marx, 1979: 213), and in the same year 1866 Whewell himself wrote a ferocious attack on Comte stung perhaps by Mill's jibe that he had never understood the basic three-state law (1988: 117–18). Mill rejected Whewell's exclusion of the scientific method from social analysis and festooned his massive study of logic with quotes from Comte only to delete after his break with Comte virtually all references to him in later editions. I am not going to examine these controversies here, or the differences between these writers on social experimentation (Brown, 1997), but rather to examine the idea Comte had of his own project in writing on the sciences as preparation for founding a new science.

Comte's project for a scientific sociology was conceived as a part of a programme of social reconstruction, a step towards designing a new polity. But there are difficulties in reading this project as Serres points out as against most other readings:

> alone of all the philosophers since Kant ... Comte laboured to acquire all the scientific knowledge of his time: he did not cheat or lie, never invented a concept which might allow him to escape this labour. In the course of this heroic philosophy, he chose from the sciences the very best models and captured the heuristic gesture of local and global science so well that he continued and concluded the itinerary of the *Encyclopédie* with the invention of a new human science ultimately conditioned by all those which had preceded it.
>
> (Serres, 1995b: 452)

The new philosophy is a philosophy not just of an order of differences but an order of the way that these differences themselves become differential (the second order differences, that is the comparison of the break between chemistry and biology with that between biology and sociology (Heilbron, 1990)). Sociology cannot apply existing methods as such since each science is methodologically innovative, and is directly subordinate to the science above it in the hierarchy of sciences and indirectly to the rest in a specific kind of spiritual tradition.

The scientific hierarchy is understood, then, in the following way: the generality of mathematics extends to all possible objects, while that of physics to all physical objects with mass and energy; the life sciences are a yet more restricted order of phenomena with social phenomena within this. So while mathematical methods are appropriate to a certain type of object-generality, biological methods are applicable to only a more restricted order, for very precise reasons which is provisionally analysed in terms of the degree of complexity of the scientific object concerned. The identification of this sequence and the theory of the differential order of the sciences is to recognise and legitimise a specific kind of scientific tradition, one that develops not spontaneously but consciously. Sociology is probably not the first to recognise these principles, but it is the first to apply them in a fully conscious way, that Comte called 'positivism' in order to create the matrix in order to give birth to itself. It is then, and pays the price for being, the first truly *reflexive* science. And the price paid has been high: its claim to legitimacy comes from the fact that it has been constructed on the basis of a certain theoretical model of the sciences, and that model was becoming rapidly outmoded. Not only do scientists themselves play only a minor role in the rapidly changing world of the sciences, but whole discipline paradigms, as Kuhn later classically argued, also seem doomed to be mere episodes in the growth of knowledge: is this the price to be paid to contribute to an intellectual discipline that is progressive? Is sociology progressive?

Conforming to the analysis of the previous sciences we would expect his project for sociology to entail the elaboration of a definition of the domain, primary and secondary laws, use of hypotheses, indirect experiment, conjectures and where necessary theoretical fictions controlled by observations and the demarcation criteria of scientificity established by his general philosophy of the sciences, developed in relation to a new fundamental theory of the domain. The role of theory is thus a paramount one, and the object of the first 'fundamental theory' in sociology was the law of the three states.

This contextualisation is important and quite different from those conventionally proposed in relation to Comte's work which is to see Comte only in relation to the ideals of 1789 or to read Comte as a naïve conservative trying to put the clock back to the Middle Ages. In fact Comte was hostile in his first intellectual career to all the regimes of his period, to absolute monarchy, constitutional monarchy, a bourgeois parliamentary republic, Bonapartism, and communism. Only later, certain in the belief that the final revolution was imminent through the joint action of the modern proletariat, and a new priesthood under the affective influence of women, did he move away from a political radicalism on the left. Saint-Simon, in search of funds, had appealed to Napoleon I directly to allow him to develop schemes appropriate to a modernising programme. Comte in his second career appealed to the Tsar of Russia, and to Napoleon III in a similar style. He never tired of describing his objective as one of searching for a 'non-subversive' way to terminate the Western Revolution. The new positive calendar which Comte drew up in 1840s dates modern time from 14th July, 1789, thus rejecting both the revolution's calendar, and Napoleon's return to the Gregorian calendar in 1804 – a simple fact which is entirely problematic in the conservative reading of Comte's position (Petit, 1991). The central argument of this position was a radical completion of the idea outlined by Saint-Simon for a theory of the system of the sciences. But the way Comte went about was regarded as utterly heretical.

COMTE'S NEW PHILOSOPHY WAS BORN AS HERESY

The first period of Comte's work is perhaps best understood as an attempt to transform the doctrine of Saint-Simon by drawing on the models and ideas of the sciences that dominated Paris in 1800 into the new scientific idiom of 'sociology', and to indicate the way to create a secular positive polity.

It is easy to identify the radical elements of Comte's early thought which are those common to the milieu of Saint-Simonianism in which he was immersed as a young intellectual, and out of which sociology and socialism were established. But when soon after 1825, the Saint-Simonian religion was being institutionalised by Bazard and Enfantin, Comte's work was immediately condemned as its first heresy, Comte its first heretic on 15th July 1829 (Iggers (ed.), 1972: 231f.) – the text of excommunication was read by his former friend Rodriques:

> if he tries to prove that devotion will be subjected to cold calculation, that imagination will soar upward only with the permission of cumbersome and obstructive reason, and that the words of the poet will go forth from his mouth only after having been commented upon, weighed and hacked to pieces by the measuring stick, the scales, and the scalpel of science, then we shall say that this man is a heretic, that he has renounced his master. (p. 233)

Against the dry scientific conceptions developed by Comte, the Saint-Simonian's held that it is artists and poets who first envision the new future:

> at this very moment the men who deserve to called poets are those to whom the secret of social destiny has been revealed … only when they have pierced the veil separating us from the future, does science, departing from this revelation as from a great hypothesis, justify this revelation through the interlinking of all past events. (pp. 240–1)

In the next lecture, read on 29th July 1829, the topic is a confession by someone who had followed the Comtean heresy but had corrected himself: 'Fortunately I stopped; *Saint-Simon held me back at the edge of the abyss*' (p. 246). The lecture is a long homily on how to bring this 'brother' Comte back into the Saint-Simonian fold.

The heresy was dangerous because pure rationalism and science demoted emotion, feeling and vision held by the cult as the true sources of regeneration. What the musicians associated with the Saint-Simonians, like Liszt and Berlioz in particular, were interested in was not simply revolutionary, transcendental technique, but new forms of expression, new musical techniques of the soul. Comte's project, which centred on one fundamental idea of a cognitive sequence, theological, metaphysical and positive, argues that in the new conjuncture it is science, not art or literature, which plays the determinant role. His milieu was that of the mathematicians and the sciences.

Comte's thesis, therefore, rests, as we have seen, on the idea that all sciences are organised around fundamental theory which defines their object and their domain, and are based on methods of observation appropriate to this domain constituted by unique and homogeneous phenomena. The detailed reading of the sciences in the Course aimed to identify the specific methods employed and developed in each of the main sciences and to understand their unity and differences. Comte's proposition is that the sciences have developed unequally because there is a structure of dependency visible in the order of appearance of these bodies of knowledge. His advocacy of a new order of philosophy, positive philosophy, is aimed to make this conscious and to begin the process of harmonisation of the sciences into a genuine system. If the sciences are dependent on one another in a certain peculiar way, this peculiarity should be understood in a new philosophical reflection. The positive philosophy is the heir to the earlier seventeenth century efforts of Bacon and Descartes, who tried to 'reconstruct the system of received ideas from top to bottom' (1975: I, 61) in *a philosophia prima* (1974b: 39, SPP, IV, 154–60). The nineteenth century will be a century like the seventeenth, capable of regenerating the whole body of the sciences by reorganising it into a second philosophy that will be able to form the matrix out of which the new science of sociology will be born.

FROM SPONTANEOUS GROWTH TO THE MATURE SYSTEM OF THE SCIENCES

Comte's account of the formation of the sciences has been read in a number of different, sometimes divergent ways. The question posed here is not whether he was the founder of the history of the sciences, but rather, more simply, to examine how he understood the way theory was essential to the constitution of any science. This question is essential in any adequate appreciation of his attempt to establish a new science within the field of the existing sciences. First of all he specifically notes that to repeat the historical order of the emergence of the sciences as an explanation of their emergence is a basic error for 'to pursue a science historically is quite a different thing from learning the history of its progress' (1974b: 43). Indeed the difference in the order of appearance of the sciences and their interior order of dependences or what he notes as their 'dogmatic order' forces the analysis into a consideration of modes of exposition (Althusser).[3] Comte claims that his account will in the main follow an order of historical exposition for reasons of accessibility, but will correct this order where necessary in the narrative. His account thus follows the order: mathematics (vol. I, 1830), astronomy, physics (vol. II, 1835), chemistry, and biology (vol. III, 1835) a certain well-defined order which reveals their intellectual dependence on each other once the sequence is started, and third, that although each science develops a methodology appropriate to its own problems, a reflection on the basic and essential unity of the scientific method emerges gradually in its own right. This can be disengaged as a new kind of philosophy – one which oversees the continuous struggle of science with metaphysical or theological concerns.

THE INTERDEPENDENCY OF THE INTELLECTUAL DISCIPLINES IN A GOVERNED SYSTEM

Comte's discussion of *mathematics* is significant because it is clear that he wants to show that this discipline is both abstract and rational on the one hand and founded in relation to concrete problems on the other: the concrete aspects of mathematics are a real natural science, while its abstract aspects are a decisive extension of natural logic. Unlike the life sciences and social sciences, Comte's view was that mathematics had reached a degree of development that it would be possible 'to arrange its different parts into a single system, in order to prepare for further advances' (CPP, cited Fraser, 1990: 251; Comte, 1851: 65). It determines 'magnitudes by each other, according to the precise relations which exist between them' (1974b: 54). Mathematics is divided into geometry and mechanics on the one hand as observational and concrete practices, while abstract mathematics includes arithmetic, algebra and calculus on the other. An important consideration is devoted to the theory of definition. He noted that a rational definition defined its object as unique, assigning a property which belonged to it alone. But this property might be of two types. The first might be 'characteristic'; the second might be 'explanatory' in the sense that it expressed a mode of the generation of the object (for example the definition of the circle). Descartes' theory of vortices was valuable for in failing it revealed that definitions should not attempt to disclose 'the primitive agents, or mode of production of phenomena, but only their laws' (1974b: 103).

At the beginning of the nineteenth century Comte thought that mathematics was regressing, was being attacked on all sides by a wave of metaphysical interventions. As a mathematics teacher and examiner, and having been trained in mathematics at the Ecole Polytechnique (his notes from courses by the leading mathematician, Cauchy for example survive (see Dhombres, in Bourdeau and Chazel, 2002 : 29), he was nevertheless even in this field an outsider; by the 1830s he was quite isolated from the leading developments. One historian has written that 'one of the most striking things about Comte's mathematical formation was that … he never had any inkling of the significance of Cauchy's analysis' (Fraser, 1990: 256). Another historian has written however of the strange stand-off between Cauchy and Comte who never directly referred to his teacher and opponent at the Polytechnique. Perhaps there was a secret rivalry between the two (Dhombres argues this was its source of vitality). Once Comte had been expelled from the Ecole, its vitality began to decline. In other words although Comte's work on mathematics was strangely uneven, for on the one hand his written presentations, leading up to the 598 pages of the *Traité Élémenaire de Géométrie Analytique* (of 1843), contained both general knowledge of the current state of the discipline, he also showed good knowledge of more advanced developments such as that of Abel and Jacobi on elliptic functions (Fraser, 1990: 251). Comte's role was one of teacher and provocateur through his constant opposition to closed-in specialisation (Dhombres, in Bourdeau and Chazel, 2002: 30).

Fraser's discussion of Comte's account shows that the specific contribution of this analysis is its new approach to calculus which is seen as a process in which such mathematical artifices are introduced to help analytical only to be eliminated at the point of calculation. Here transcendental analysis is conceived as the calculus of indirect functions. His analysis does not suggest that the logic of empirical enumeration is the primary base for mathematics, but rather that it is through abstraction that genuine analytic expressions become a basis for investigations into observable, empirical relations between phenomena. These analytic expressions use the resources from the concrete domains of mathematics, and supplement them with specific kinds of imaginary devices, fictions, and artifices to facilitate the formation of equations which determine the calculation of quantitative relations between phenomena. Mathematics is the practice of approaching 'all the quantities which any phenomena can present as connected and interwoven with one another, with the view of deducing them from one another' (Comte, 1851: 71).

It is in this manner that Comte was able to argue that all accounts which consider mathematics as developing independently of observation were purely metaphysical. Equally metaphysical were all positions in mechanics which endeavoured to find hidden ontological origins for things, as was the case in d'Alembert, rather than from direct observation. This is why he thought highly of the work of Lagrange, arguing that he took 'the science of abstract mechanics to the highest degree of logical perfection – that is, to a rigorous unity' (1974b: 127). Comte held that although mechanics was based on observation it is only brought into a coherent state of knowledge through the elaboration of the artifice of 'virtual velocities' introduced and then cancelled in the analysis of motion, in a way comparable to that in calculus. Archimedes established the statics and Galileo dynamics, while Lagrange brought the two sides of mechanics together; by interposing the idea of virtual momentum and virtual velocity in the analysis of forces acting on a point he was able to work out the method of determining equilibrium. He criticised Lagrange's approach to dynamics arguing that a 'dynamic consideration really consists in conceiving any varied motion as compounded, each moment, of a certain uniform motion and another uniformly varied – likening it to the vertical motion of a heavy body under a first impulsion … (this) removes the limits within which we suppose ourselves to be confined by disclosing to us in an abstract way, a much more perfect measure of all varied motion' (1974b: 125). The significant distinction latent in this discussion is between the genuinely based scientific notions of fictional artifices, essential to scientific reasoning, and what he calls 'the fantastic discussions of the metaphysicians' that posit abstract entities beyond the data of sensory experience (Fraser, 1990: 254).

It is clear from this, and from other interventions that Comte's relation to scientific practice was essentially one of conjecture, rectification, improvement, harmonisation. This can be interpreted in two ways. Michel Serres for example concluded in his early writings on Comte, that this practice was above all an attempt to protect a declining position in mathematics, the position of Lagrange certainly dominant in 1800, and still in a revised form influential in the nineteenth century up to the work of Mach in the 1880s. Others on the other hand interpret Comte as engaging in more of a particular kind of response to new developments that were in line with his overall project of resisting what he saw as the resurgence of metaphysics. The moral regeneration of mathematics was an element of Comte's ambitions from an early date. The discussion in the Course, then, even on mathematics was not an attempt to present a balance sheet in any neutral manner, a kind of snapshot of the current state of the disciplines. Science is a battlefield; Comte is a protagonist in the field. This involves him in attempts to develop positions in what he sees as the frontline controversies as a scientist himself. It also involves him in critiques of positions he sees as retrogressive, risking 'underestimating the possibilities' in new developments (Fraser, 1990: 155). Comte allied himself to thinkers and traditions not only because he thought them technically progressive: he advocated the positions of Lagrange for example because it also developed a certain new kind of reflexivity (1974b: 496).

In the end, Comte's introductory book on geometry was not taken up as a teaching textbook, or standard reference in France, and his mathematics has been adjudged tautological: 'It was hardly satisfactory to suggest that concrete mathematics derived from the phenomena relations that were then analyzed by arithmetic and algebra. The concepts and results of the latter were presumably involved in the original derivation' (Fraser, 1990: 255). Later his forays into physics were also criticised on methodological grounds (Pickering 1993: 452). But it could be that Comte was engaged in another order of reflection, the construction of the idea of space in geometry as a site of 'semantic transformations', primarily a philosophical not mathematical reflection (Dhombres, in ibid.: 37, 77). In practice, Comte 'provided a philosophical reinterpretation of Lagrange's mathematics that adapted it to the needs of phenomenal empirical science, thereby establishing the basic orientation of nineteenth-century positivist physics' particularly in the 1830s the molecular physics of Poisson, and later in the century (Fraser, 1990: 255).

Comte defines *astronomy* as the domain of laws of the 'geometrical and mechanical phenomena presented the heavenly bodies' or rather more specifically those bodies which belong to the solar system (1974b: 133). This discipline became a science at the point when the observations accumulated over millennia – the true germ of positivity – were connected with the geometrical theories of the Greeks. It functioned like all sciences to secure accurate prediction of future events. Having looked at the role of radically new instruments of observation, and the difference between refraction and parallax, he once again divides the discussion into a statics and a dynamics of the solar system. The first of these, for example, raises the question of the earth, its size and form, and these can be calculated through indirect proofs. The second considers geometrical theory and the planetary motion, and the theory of gravitation. In this discussion Comte argues that astronomy is fundamentally dependent on mathematics, and no other science. And to the surprise of many readers, including Hayek, he argues that all the other sciences in their turn are dependent on the path breaking discoveries of astronomy, even sociology. Crucially, he argues, it was astronomy which decentred the whole order of superstitions of essences and eliminated the resort in explanation to ultimate causes; these notions were replaced with that of necessary conditions of existence. The theory of gravity displaced the theological notion that divine beings held the universe together. This great reversal, this great 'humiliation' of the divine will and the central position of humanity in relation to it was achieved through a mechanics dependent on geometry, a purely cumulative relation with no reciprocity. It is a rule he concludes that more general phenomena rule the most particular without being in any degree reciprocally influenced for it was Newton and not Descartes who founded celestial mechanics, because Descartes had been seduced into searching for ultimate 'modes of production', the origin, of the phenomena (1974b: 169).

The sciences are established in a hierarchy and do not engage in balanced or equal exchanges. There is accumulation, but it is not the incremental accumulation of detail. There are profound metaphysical crises resolved in theoretical revolutions, and they may be blocked by the intervention of regressive theological forces. The new philosopher begins to lay down the rules for the scope of astronomy: as a science it must be limited to its field of observation. As this field is the solar system itself, the study of the universe has no place in 'natural philosophy' and is 'excluded from positive philosophy' (1974b: 158). Where there are no adequate methods of observing a phenomenon a field of conjecture will open up where any theory is as plausible as any other. In relation to the nature of the solar system, which can be regarded as a completely determined system of 'invariable relations', calculations based on probabilities are inappropriate (1975: I, 435). Clearly for Comte, astronomy (his *Traité Philosophique d'Astronomie Populaire* was republished in 1985 in a series edited by Latour) seems to be a science nearing completion. His lectures on astronomy were very popular, attracting audiences of some hundreds. He held them at times that would clash with church services.

Physics and chemistry are, in Comte's analysis, to be distinguished by three considerations. The object of physics is the more general of the two, it relates to the mass of objects, and it does not descend to the examination of molecules when bodies change their composition – this is the sphere of chemistry (1974b: 193–4). The method of studying these sciences, in fact he says 'the only way', is to start with an idea of the science in a perfect, ideal state and then to study the fundamental difficulties presented by this ideal perfection.' (1974b: 195). Physics begins to encounter objects that are more complex than those in astronomy, but this is an encounter where direct experimentation becomes possible. He defines an experiment as 'placing bodies in artificial conditions, expressly instituted to enable us to examine the action of the phenomena … under a particular point of view' (1974b: 195). Physics permits the application of mathematical ideas, whereas chemistry does not. If astronomy opened the contest between theology and science, it is on the ground of physics that the principal battles have been fought out.

The crucial contribution of physics to scientific method however, has been the practice of construction of genuine hypotheses, for there are:

> only two general modes by which we can get at the laws of any phenomenon – immediate analysis of the course of the phenomenon, or its relation to some more extended law already established; in other words by induction or deduction … Neither of these methods would help … if we did not begin by anticipating the results … altogether conjectural in the first instance, with regard to some of the very notions which are the object of the inquiry. Hence the necessary introduction of hypotheses.
>
> (1974b: 199)

But the introduction of hypotheses is not productive without the introduction of suitable controls. In essence hypotheses must conform to the trial of verifiability. They are kinds of anticipation which in other circumstances might be observed immediately. This is a key line of demarcation between science and non-science. In the former, scientific work attempts to 'confirm or invalidate' hypotheses. In metaphysics, the very formulation of the question makes controversy irresolvable and interminable. Explanation by appeal to invisible or intangible entities is strictly outside of any scientific domain, since all investigation into the 'production' of the phenomenon ex nihilo is 'altogether beyond the nature of our faculties'. Such hypotheses only conjure 'fantastic notions' for example about the 'ether' in fluids, light, heat – an entity that is 'invisible, intangible, even imponderable, and inseparable from the substances which they activate' (1974b: 201). These metaphysical elements are as unscientific as any theological explanation which has recourse to angels, genii, and spirits (p. 201). Science therefore should confine 'hypotheses to the yet unknown circumstances of phenomena, or their yet hidden laws' (1974b: 201).

In the process of the construction of physics as a scientific domain, the elimination of metaphysical entities in explanation has been a protracted and complex process. His discussion considers this process in the science of the weight of solids and liquids, heat, sound, light and electricity, at the end of which he concludes his 'business has been to carry on a philosophical operation … that of disengaging real science from the influence of the old metaphysical philosophy': the main barriers and obstacles encountered were either attempts to explain the primal origin of the phenomena, or an 'excessive systematisation' brought about when mathematics is introduced inappropriately (p. 247).

Comte defines *chemistry* as the science which deals with the 'laws of the phenomena of composition and decomposition, which result from the molecular and specific mutual action of different substances, natural or artificial' (1974b: 252). Here observation and experimentation are given full reign for the first time. There is an introduction also of the analytic series 'in which a phenomenon shall be modified more and more, whether by successive simplifications or graduations' (p. 254). The analysis may be completed by analysis or synthesis, decomposition or re-composition. Chemistry is another battlefield. The main problem in the constitution of scientific reason here was the metaphysical conception of chemical affinity. He describes these affinities as 'mere reproduction(s) in abstract terms, of the statement of the phenomenon' (p. 258). The science of chemistry only begins to emerge when it establishes 'exact relations … among observed facts, allowing the deduction of the most extensive series of secondary phenomena form the smallest number of original phenomena' (p. 259). The greatest methodological contribution of this science is towards the rational construction of nomenclature (p. 260).

But chemistry still awaits a rational systematisation and until that is achieved there is difficulty in defining its true limits. The account charts the significant power struggle over the possession of a domain. In crucial respects even the idea of an 'organic chemistry' rests on confusion (p. 262). Only glimpses of an established domain can be caught here and there in such theories as the principle of definite proportions, or electrochemical theory. He takes an example of a law such as the theory of saline decomposition – 'two soluble salts, of any kind, mutually decompose each other whenever their reaction may produce an insoluble salt or one less soluble than the other' (p. 272). If Comte were the empiricist he is often assumed to be, we might expect him to be satisfied with a proposition of invariance of this kind. But he remarks that law is fundamentally without scientific force, since it is disconnected from any general law of the domain. No genuine law can be explanatory other than by showing that 'it enters into another more general than itself' (p. 272). Chemistry will only become a science when it combines the study of organic and inorganic substances.

There are all kinds of (epistemological) obstacles that have to be overcome: arbitrary classifications, violation of 'essential analogies', failure to generalise a progressive doctrine across its full range of phenomena. He picks up in particular the damaging consequences following the intervention of chemists in the analysis of physiology: it meant that these questions 'were taken possession of by the chemists, who annexed them to their own domain' (p. 294). The argument leads him to plead for the liberation of biology from chemistry at essential points, especially where there are questions of anatomy and physiology. He stresses the biological conception of elements of the organism

(Blainville) against its simple products. Indeed it is not really a question of liberating biology but of a true subordination of chemistry to biological theory in this realm, just as mathematics had to be subordinate to physics in its domain.

Biology, which is to be the immediate precursor of sociology in this series, is defined by reference to its object and to its domain. Its object is the domain of living organisms, or more precisely 'of connecting in both a general and a specific manner, the double idea of organ and medium with that of function' or connecting the anatomical and the physiological point of view, the organism in its environment (*milieu*) (p. 308). Unlike chemistry, biology is concerned with organised bodies. Its domain is the study of all possible organisms with the aim of understanding human biology. He examines the methodological procedures of observation peculiar to biology: the creation of special instruments, new forms of experimentation, comparative analysis, and pathological analysis. Attention is drawn to the introduction of hypotheses, especially in the investigation of hidden functions. He also draws attention to the difference between the practice of 'imagining a series of hypothetical cases' in mathematics, and the construction of hypotheses. But the latter is 'entirely different, inasmuch as in the latter case the solution alone is imaginary; whereas in the former, the problem itself is radically ideal.' He suggests that in the analysis of 'comparative biology … the process would be to intercalate, among known organisms, certain purely fictitious organisms … rendering the biological series more homogeneous and continuous' (p. 327). He observes: 'whenever it is adopted it will constitute perhaps another ground of relation between biology and mathematics' (p. 328).

Comte then reflects on the possibility of perfecting biology as a way of revealing obstacles to its development. The prospect is opened he says for the completion of the theory of classification, a true biological hierarchy (p. 328), for:

> each of the fundamental sciences has … as we have seen the exclusive property of specially developing one of the great logical procedures of which the whole positive method is composed; and it is thus that the more complex, while dependent on the simpler, react on their superiors by affording them new rational powers and instruments. (p. 330)

His consideration of biology notes the fact that although the discovery of the function of the heart and the law of gravity were achieved at the same time, the subsequent uneveness of development of the two disciplines is remarkable. For Comte:

> such a difference cannot be attributed wholly to the greater complexity of physiological phenomena, and must have depended much also on the scientific spirit which directed their general study – on the one hand, the supposed organic chemistry, a bastard study … and, on the other hand, vague, incoherent … metaphysical doctrines … The barren anarchy which has resulted from so vicious an organisation of scientific labour would be enough of itself to testify to the direct utility of the general, yet positive point of view … (p. 368).

Much of the analysis of biology in these pages is prescriptive. At one crucial point he opens an examination of the tissue theory of the famous biologist Bichat. In the search for a viable basis for the identification of pathologies Bichat had investigated the relation between diseased tissues and organs to find no clear correlation. He identified twenty-one tissue types, and organs were made up, he thought, out of the tissues combined in them. Some tissues had vital properties, others simple physical properties. Just as with phrenology, also keenly supported by Comte for attempting to locate thinking and affective processes in the brain, Bichat was attempting to locate life properties in the tissue structures. Comte however was suspicious that lurking here was a survival of metaphysical vitalism, but in a context that could be radicalised to form the basic elements of the new science if the comparative method was introduced. Just like his intervention in phrenology, he introduced his own classification of tissues, suggesting that all tissues grew out of, or were modifications of a single type of tissue: 'the fundamental unity of the organic world requires that all types of tissue are derived by more and more complex transformations from a single primitive tissue' (cited in McCormick, 1974: 82). The basic tissue he called 'cellular' or 'generator' – or we might today think of something like 'stem'. He then introduced his own terminology for types of tissues that were to become structure (sclerous, kystrous) and tissues that were to grow in combination with fundamental tissue to become muscle or nervous tissue (fibrine, neurine). In fact, as McCormick suggests: 'Comte does not explain the nature of these special 'elements' nor does he discuss how their combination with tissue takes place' (p. 83). What Comte here seeks to undertake is a critical reworking of terminology and basic classificatory terms, in order for biology to work itself free from the most dangerous theoretical metaphysical temptation in biology: vitalism. And behind this is another objective: to secure biology's relative independence as a science from chemistry. Here he launched a direct attack on Bichat's idea that all tissues contained the properties of 'sensibility' and 'irritability'. For Comte only organisms with a nervous system could respond to stimuli in this way. It is not surprising that historians allow Comte not only a significant role in establishing the very term biology, but also of having played a crucial role in its modern development (Canguilhem, 1981: 93ff., 1983: 61ff.).

6

But Why Did Comte Need Sociology?

Comte announced in his writings of the 1820s that he was committing himself to a programme of works, the completion of which would be essential to avert 'long and terrible convulsions' in modern society (1974a: 137). The programme had identified three series of works: a study of the 'general progress of the human intellect destined to become the basis of a positive polity'; a series which would establish 'a complete system of Positive Education'; and third a 'general exposition of the Collective Action which civilised men … can exercise over Nature' (p. 138).

Comte's demonstration of the legitimacy and the necessity of the new social science to be located in the system of the sciences occupied him from the first to the third volume, of six, of the *Course in Positive Philosophy* (1830 to 1839). Only in volume four (1839) did he begin in earnest to discuss the foundation of social science, and to define the scope of sociology. In the first three volumes he had discussed the formations of the sciences, in their order of appearance and consolidation, and in their interdependences within this order. His discussion is often taken as a kind of summary of the results of the sciences, or even a manual. Even in the version presented in English in the 1850s by Harriet Martineau some sections were omitted as being out of date, an argument which appears even in the introduction to the current French edition (Serres suggests the work was already completely out of date on its appearance, in Comte,

1975: I, x). But, more recently as has been argued by Heilbron (1995), the work was an attempt at quite a different project: to analyse the order of appearance and interdependencies of the sciences, to analyse the way in which they constituted their domains of investigation, their theoretical programmes and methods, their internal divisions, and suggest ways in which they could be organised into a systematic whole. But above all of course the aim was to legitimise the methods by which the new science of society could be founded. He needed to work out and present its first methodological rules, and to present its first rational findings (this work took Comte between 1839 and 1842) within the system of the accumulated scientific tradition. Before looking at the specific forms of observation he proposed for sociology that it was necessary to examine the way he thought theory controlled a scientific practice.

Comte needed to invent and develop the complex discipline of sociology: in order to demonstrate the necessity of and contribute the decisive link between the 'positive' rising series and the new political organisation. He first expressed this heretically as a new spiritual power of intellectuals ('savants'), but this was only to claim that it was work in science and scientific philosophy that was the key to making things happen. First of all Comte believed that among the large number of causes of social evolution there is a preponderant one namely what he calls intellectual or 'fundamental opinions' (1975: II, 210). The introduction of a new method, properly controlled, maintains the analytical focus on the interconnectedness of social developments through constant comparisons across the range of social activities. The law of the social itself arises *theoretically* in relation to the facts of human nature as given by biology to sociology; it is 'possible to conceive *a priori* all the fundamental relations between phenomena, independently of any direct exploration' and for speculation then to be controlled by historical induction (1975: II, 212). But what is the theory? In fact Comte resists a new statement and is content, surprisingly, to repeat in 1839 a formula he had already conceived in 1822:

> the constant succession of three states, first theological, second metaphysical and finally positive, through which our intellect passes in every field of speculation.
>
> (1975: II, 211)

This is a law of invariant logical connection. In fact Comte does not (in presenting the law here in this chapter (51)) actually proceed in this order of analysis. He adopts an order of theoretical analysis which breaks fundamentally with a descriptive empirical history. It is theoretically constituted in a specific way and the exposition in this chapter (Chapter

4 in 1974b) confirms the philosophical order – first, theological, second the third state, positive, and third the second state, the metaphysical. Comte explains this order later in the chapter as arising from the necessity in science of constructing the extreme terms of the analysis *before* the analysis of the intermediary term (1975: II, 225). In effect the key to the analysis lies in the conception of the positive state itself. Far from being achieved even in the intellectual sphere (Comte had already noted that his own Course itself was the only completely positive work in the social sciences), the general 'tendency' towards positivism had only recently been definitively established (1974b: 531). Thus what we have is an *a priori* law (the inevitable progress of reason), the historical method, one which establishes an abstract line of development, constructed in relation to extreme terms (one in the past and one in the future) to produce an analysis of current society and politics in order to define the conflicting alliances within the metaphysical state.

This might seem to be a series of sleights of hand, which inevitably give rise to misunderstandings. But the gravest misunderstanding of all is that which occurs when Comte undertakes the actual exposition of the law chapter by chapter. Here he produces not the philosophical order but the 'historical' chronological sequence; what is almost always read as a law expressing a concrete sequence (fetishism, polytheism, monotheism, metaphysics, positivism), is actually a misreading of the law itself. The exposition of the Course is a sequence of chapters as follows: fetishism, polytheism, monotheism, metaphysical state I (the decomposition of monotheism), metaphysical state II (the rise of positivism) – and then a final chapter in the sequence actually steps out of the historical method, into a directly empirical analysis of the French Revolution as a further stage leading up to the positive state. The confusion over this sequence arises as a failure to understand its method of construction, and paradoxically failure to identify the slippage in Comte's practice from the abstract to the concrete in the same 'series' – a violation of his own methodological precepts that he continued to make throughout his work. I take it as a basic rule in reading Comte to distinguish between objects which have a known existence and those that have a purely theoretical and fictional future existence, even if Comte himself refers to future states being better known than current ones. Yet few readers have taken this elementary precaution.

We have seen that in 1820 Comte had already worked up an account of the 'general character of modern history' dividing up his material into two series of social facts, the decline series and the rising series. When he came to present and discuss his sociological methods, it was the 'historical method' which loomed large, but this was only one of the methods he elaborated. The historical method itself had yet to be founded within the frame of the system of the sciences.

METHOD

Comte proposed to begin the construction of the new science of sociology by using the way that sciences depend on former sciences as both resources and controls. As biology is subordinate to chemistry and even mathematics in a certain way, so the new sociology will be in the same way dependent on biology and can learn from the way in which the earlier sciences established themselves. In order to achieve the foundation of the new discipline sociologists have to be competent in the other sciences, their logics, their methods, and to be competent in the new philosophy which considers the law of their uneven development and the structure of their interrelations. Positive philosophy, thus understood, is the attempt to regulate the system of the sciences (some are still isolated outside the system), and to produce the conditions for the emergence of new sciences. It also in its regulation of the system tries to prevent certain anarchic and dispersive tendencies: in other words it aims to govern knowledge.

If we call the formation of the scientific imagination the development of theoretical logics of the sciences, it is clear that for Comte these are only strictly possible in so far as they are controlled by the limits imposed by the world as produced through observation: thus the fundamental rule is that imagination is subordinate to observation. In this practice Comte embarks on the presentation of the main methods of observation open to a social science. Clearly these methods cannot be a simple application of any one set of methods from an established science. The sciences do not simply imitate each other as simulacra, but must guided by and subordinated to the nearest science in the hierarchy. Thus he rules out as inappropriate the direct intervention of methods of the natural sciences and draws on those developed by biology, while being aware that sociology will make its own contribution to methodology. In the discussion of methods of observation in sociology, Comte identifies four principal approaches to the art of observation (1975: II, 141ff.): the direct observation of social phenomena, indirect experimentation, comparison, and the historical method. These methods do not work on their own account, for this would only lead to an infinite dispersion. They work under the aegis of the fundamental theory which determines the object a domain of sociology itself. This sets up, as it does in biology the apparent vicious circle of an emerging science, that it has to fashion its theory and its methods of observation both at the same, time – that is it has to produce in one act its hypothesis in relation to its observations, and its observations from its hypothesis. This vicious circle if not controlled could also connect bad theory with incoherent observation. The rational theories developed must remain under constant rectification (Comte 1974b: 139–41).

The domain of observation is that of 'social facts'. The study of social facts is only significant if they are brought together in explanation, otherwise they remain purely isolated phenomena. Observation must be subordinated to the theory of social states or the succession of states. This first division of the sociological domain is a first step to organising observations which must always proceed from the system to the elements (1975: II, 141; 1974b: 476). The only way in which these can be started initially is a systematic training of observers and the development of a genuine theoretical culture built on a rational education. Direct observation will be possible leading to the direct description of customs and events. If the interconnectedness of things is at first an obstacle, it later makes possible the rapid connection of concrete observations with the highest abstract scientific notions.

The second 'fundamental mode of the art of observation' (1975: II, 142) is that of experimentation. If the impossibility of any direct control of the elements rules out conventional forms of experimentation indirect forms are evident. These exist where the elements of a structure vary naturally. As in biology it is the incidence of naturally occurring forms of pathology which constitutes the equivalent of direct experimentation. In sociology, pathology occurs where the normal forms of solidarity or succession are perturbed. This occurs in the exceptional abnormalities of revolutionary epochs. The analysis of such pathologies has never been subjected to genuine scientific control, yet only by subjecting analysis to such control can the results become reliable. Until the work of Broussais, pathological facts were thought to be the outcome of the suspension of law. It is essential to regard pathological facts as perturbations of a normal state, the equivalent of modifications brought about by secondary causes. Thus the domain of sociological facts should be divided into normal and pathological facts, in an exact analogy with biological illness and this can be done only through the effective control of theory in either statics or dynamics, and within any order of sociology – practical, intellectual, moral or political (1975: II, 144).

The third kind of observation proceeds through structured comparison. Even though there is a prejudice of comparing human with animal societies, this should not be ruled out. It has the advantage besides of making analysis relative not absolute. But evidently the main orders of comparison should be within the sociological domain itself. That is between different societies, and within the same society. Within the same society such as France it is possible to compare the states of civilisation of the different classes, since especially in the intellectual realm there are 'more or less faithful representatives of almost all degrees of development' as can be found in the different societies across the globe (ibid.: 146). But intermediary phases of evolution may have left almost no trace and in these cases only indirect observation is possible under the control of theory. But problems exist for the analyst concerning the distinction between real and apparent filiations, between principal and secondary developments, how to learn from comparisons between divergent but distinct varieties of human society. The initial key to sociological analysis is the development of an initial general conception, but rational and scientific, of social development. Without such theory observation becomes a 'systematic empiricism' (1975: II, 148). Having prepared the matrix, he then turns to the most important of his new methods.

The fourth mode of observation is in effect merely an extension of the comparative method: the historical method, which is the only rational basis for a new and adequate system of political logic. It is this method which really distinguishes sociology from that of other sciences. It studies the influence of cultural dependencies as they arise and are transmitted from one human generation to another. It provides the fundamental verification of the sociological point of view by proceeding in a new way, from the whole to the part, holistically in the light of a conception of social evolution. In the absence of this requirement historical analysis becomes fragmented and sterile, limited to one country or one century. It is only a special kind of scientific history which puts facts into controlled and co-ordinated complete analytic series, and studies their interconnectedness and dependencies (ibid.: 150). In effect the demands of this method conflict with demands which restrict analysis to the present believing that the past is of little interest. One way of mastering this kind of method is to undertake exercises which attempt from an analysis of antecedents to predict outcomes (ibid.: 152), for the predictions of future states are only possible if the past is also predictable (virtual history: Ferguson, 1998). A genuinely scientific sociology analyses the ensemble of social facts, as they are continuous into the present from a perspective determined by a future state. And all these speculative analyses must be consistent with the known laws of other sciences. The historical method is one which shows that in the relation between two successive systems (disposition) the continuous growth of the progressive system is combined with the decline of the former. The main problem with this method of observation is that in studying a movement of development or decline it is essential to distinguish as in mathematics a series of continuous variations with that of a series of unlimited variations. Thus in the historical method, such a series of variations must be controlled by the general laws of human nature.[1]

This brief summary of the presentation of the main forms of observation in sociology indicates some of the principal aspects of Comte's approach: its definition of the field of social facts, the insistence that explanation is internal to these facts (the connection of social fact to other social facts), the division of the domain into socio-statics (synchronic analysis), and socio-dynamics (diachronic analysis), and to a division between normal and pathological facts. The comparative method is applicable across the range of sociology. The historical method is essentially the method of reconstructing the sequence of social evolution through its various stages. Comte suggests that this method is new. It is not a simple, purely descriptive account of historical events. It is a scientific history, a rational and normal history, constructed through the elaboration of homogeneous sequences or series across the range of human activities (practical, intellectual, moral and political). It is a historical law arising from multiple causes (primary causes from within societies and secondary causes from the social environment). Because it is so determined it can be the object of scientific prediction. Comte in fact insists that any analysis restricted to purely current phenomena is radically insufficient in sociological terms; analysis only has a value if it is linked to rational predictions and an adequate analysis of the past.

The point of Comte's recourse to the historical method and the other precautions and preparations in method, is to be in a position to establish genuine explanations. An empirical order is one thing; a theoretical and analytical construction is another. In the latter, science makes its objects appear by methods that are unique to its practice. The 'historical method' is defined as one which produces a single abstract series; these facts are disengaged then from empirical history. Comte is quite explicit in his method: it must disregard all exceptional events, and details, as lying outside of the abstractly constructed history which concentrates only on established general phenomena (1974b: 542), producing an account that is not to be confused with the concrete histories of specific societies. Sociology, then, can be conceived in this perspective as a vast process of transformation of the fragmented historical materials before it, 'each portion of this material being carefully prepared by stripping off from it whatever is peculiar or irrelevant – all circumstances, for instance, of climate, locality, etc. – in order to transfer it from the concrete to the abstract' (1974b: 543). In the analysis so constructed, says Comte, this treatment of history establishes in the abstract genealogy the new markers as signposts, 'jalons fondamentaux' (1975: II, 241) along the ideal route taken by Humanity that turns out to be one that is characterised by profound division, revolution and conflict.[2] The development of a concrete sociological series, a new type of history, is not possible until the abstract one is completed. Thus Comte completely reverses expectations. A concrete sociology is more complex than an abstract one since it has to combine elements together and these are not yet rationally available from a simple empirical enquiry.

Nevertheless there are temptations to proceed too quickly and Comte warns the reader just once: 'if the novelty and difficulty of my creative task should compel me occasionally to desert my own logical precept, the warning I have now given will enable the reader to rectify any errors into which I may lapse' (1974b: 544). We are warned, for example, that because the abstract series is not an account of any one country or people, burdened with peculiarities, it follows that without further 'concrete' analyses no direct application of any of its theoretical laws would ever be possible.

THE BIRTH OF SOCIOLOGY AS A DISCIPLINE IN THE MATRIX OF THE SCIENCES

The introduction to the science of social statics in the Course was however to be inauspicious. Comte outlines his discussion as divided between the individual, the family and society as a whole (in the later study, the System the division was different, as I shall discuss below), so the reader is thrown into an investigation of the science of phrenology today at best regarded as a proto-science. It is certainly curious that for all Comte's rigorous preparation the sociology should begin with an aspect of the subject which is in territorial and epistemological dispute, for it is clear that phrenology, is analogous to the category of organic chemistry (torn between opposing disciplines, chemistry and biology). And some of the first disputes over Comte's analysis occurred precisely because of the contentious demarcation of phrenology, psychology, ethology, and the social in the sociological domain itself. This dispute continues today in the relation between social psychology, psychoanalysis, and sociology. It is not possible to put phrenology permanently aside, since it returns to play a crucial role in Comte's later work.

The sociological investigation proper however starts, not with the individual, but with an analysis of the family, which from the point of view of the modern reader is inauspicious, since it is here Comte presents a completely uncritical view of the eternal inevitability of the patriarchal family with a notorious statement that women are in a state of 'perpetual infancy' (1974b: 504). The chapter presents some very quick sketches of the genealogy of family forms, and of marriage. The theoretical interest of this chapter lies elsewhere. Comte argues, in first proposition that the social relations in the family are based on a *union* (p. 509), while that of society is based on cooperative association (pp. 502–15). He argues that on account of the structure of intimacies, the natural hierarchies established in a limited number of relations, 'the domestic connection is of a totally different nature' from the wider patterns of association (p. 509). There are aspects of the relations established in the family permanent functions and subordinations which suggest that it is utopian ever to expect great fundamental changes here. In effect Comte idealises in a conservative fashion the eternal divisions of sex and age, in reproduction, socialisation and moral transmission through the generations, in an institution governed by unchanging natural forms of hierarchy.

It is to the principle of the division of labour that Comte really enunciates his second sociological proposition, which presents the paradox of society in a dramatic way: it is the continuous process of re-dividing the human labour process which gives rise to the essential bonds of social solidarity and which becomes the elementary cause of the growth and extent of the social organism (1975: II, 194; 1974b: 510). The *union*, the family, is not the site of a process of such increasing complexity; it is only when the division of labour becomes established on a regular basis that society is constituted in consistent and stable *associations*. It is from extending the principle of sympathy to the realm of the social that an ideal type of the social emerges in the principle that each social function should match an exact distribution of the diversity of individual human capacities, a dream which can however never be realised in any complex society where discipline and organisation are far more artificial and imperfect than in the domestic sphere. The principles of specialisation and the dispersion of occupations and activities bring into play involuntary and unplanned dependencies which affect not only individuals and classes but also arise between different peoples and which extend eventually across the globe.

Comte contrasts the principle of the process of the division of labour with its continuous tendency to specialisation and dispersion, with the third fundamental proposition: the principle of *government* itself, which rests on the spontaneously generated tendencies to regulate the various parts produced in this social process. This process establishes a new function generated at the level of the process of the whole, indeed an effect of the whole on its parts either directly or indirectly. Against a tendency to dispersion towards anarchy, the new function of government arises to regulate either the intellectual divisions which through the tendency to specialism becomes hostile even to general philosophy, or the temporal and material divisions which have gone much further and are the basic cause of the decomposition of the old order in Europe. Any reconstruction arises in relation to the spontaneously generated effects of the whole on parts which have become so dispersed that they present dangerous effects of isolation from and indifference to society itself.

The spontaneous tendency towards government leads Comte to formulate a complementary thesis (a basic principle of sociological statics): the law of the spontaneous subordination of the more detailed and specialised to the more general function; or, as Comte expresses it: 'the diverse kinds of particular operations place themselves naturally under the continuous direction of those in the next degree of generality immediately above them' (1975: II, 198). In effect, this is the theorem of the principle of the division of labour itself – each new specialisation in any human labour whenever it becomes clearly separate becomes more specific in function than the one before it and to which it is subordinate. This law is implied in the development of the sciences itself. But it is more general and develops extensively in industrial societies. It is most clearly evident in military societies where the principle is exploited to maximum effect. But this raises the question, of the relation between the concept of spontaneous social subordination and political subordination – the 'indispensable basis of government' correctly conceived (ibid.: 199). Government is the highest degree of generality in any social hierarchy. The development of government corresponds to the new and increasing inequalities produced in this process, both material and moral. In the family the development of different abilities is strictly contained, whereas in society greater differences are produced where the division of labour is extensive. There are important aspects to note in the comparison of intellectual and material hierarchies. In the latter accumulation through simple addition, and concentrations can emerge mechanically by combining small quantities; it is quite different with respect to moral or intellectual hierarchies, where no amount of combination of mediocre quantities can lead to the emergence of new qualities.

The ideas presented in the analysis here however are fundamental, if modestly presented. It is clear that the fundamental idea in Comtean sociology is that only two types or principles of sociation are evident in the sociological domain: *union* and *association*. Society is located principally in the effects of the laws of the division of labour which are two-fold: the first is the law of tendency to specialisation and detail, the second is the law of spontaneous hierarchy and subordination the basis of all government. The theory of government is based on the spontaneous effects (through the structure of dependencies) of the whole on the parts in an organism, and gives rise to a special function and organ at its highest degree of generality. The order of the appearance of the specialised fields of human knowledge is in effect determined by these laws of social solidarity. What seems surprising in this analysis is that Comte makes reference to military organisations, but does not introduce here any distinction between counsel and command discussed elsewhere, nor any distinctions concerning forms of government. Comte's interest in abnormal forms concern the division of labour taken beyond certain limits and misconceived attempts to model social on domestic forms in various utopian schemes.

7

A Sociological Theory of Modernity

After his death in 1825 Saint-Simon's legacy was divided between Comte and his school on the one hand and the 'Saint-Simonians' – led by Bazard and Enfantin on the other. It was the latter that from 1825 began to evolve the doctrines which produced in a messianic framework, the first theories of economic 'exploitation of man by man' that so influenced Marx and Engels. Comte was 'excommunicated' from this new religious movement. In fact his nervous breakdown occurred just at the moment the new doctrine was coming into being. As soon as he was able to assess it, he claimed that no such programme had ever been conceived by Saint-Simon himself, that the leaders had barely known Saint-Simon, and that the result was merely a parody of Catholicism. There is no hint in the early Comte that his solution to the problems facing France and modern Europe involved a return to religion directly; rather that religion would lose out to science. Indeed in 1817 Comte (1970: 95–6) actually proposed a law requiring all new ordinations to the priesthood should require successful passage through an examination in the sciences. In this way the priesthood would become positive.

But it is very clear in reading Comte that his alienation from the post-revolutionary political and social forms in France was profound and bitter. He had been a leader of the student revolt at the Ecole Polytechnique in Paris in 1816, and placed for a time under police surveillance. Gradually under the mentorship of Saint-Simon he worked towards a critique of the post-revolutionary settlements that has a distinct orientation: it was not polarised towards literature and the humanities, or a religious renaissance. From his intellectual base in the camp of the scientists, the mathematicians, and epistemologists, he expressed contempt not only for the unreconstructed priesthood, but also for the class he saw as producing the negative philosophy of the eighteenth century – literary culture, retrograde politicians, journalists and lawyers. Even his base, the sciences, was, according to his own reading, contaminated by its internal anarchy and the way that key scientists flirted with metaphysics (particularly theories of probability in mathematics) and his opposition to individualism in politics was mirrored by his opposition to probability theory in mathematics: both were immoral. In effect, Comte was pretty much on his own working in relative isolation, and as he admitted in a solitary manner.

In his essay on the 'Spiritual Power' published in three parts between December 1825 and February 1826 Comte, now out of the direct supervision of Saint-Simon, had begun to identify in his own terms just what was wrong with modern society. Fundamentally, he argued, the decay of spiritual authority had left society without any moral consensus (1998: 196). The evidence for this could be identified in the appearance of four symptoms – a radical 'mental anarchy', an 'almost total absence of public morality', the rise to ascendancy of 'the purely material point of view' (in England especially), and, finally, a new modern type of 'autocracy' that, he argued has 'no precise analogy at all in history'. This new kind of autocracy manifested itself above all as a new type of 'administrative despotism'. This state of affairs was characterised by a new coupling: an intensified centralisation of power and 'systematized corruption' (1998: 199). These symptoms were presented in an order that reflected he said 'their mutual dependence': the collapse of the intellectual and then the moral order. This decomposition of constraints releases, second, a generalised materialistic culture. Third, in order for society to maintain itself as a coherent body, a new kind of administrative order comes into being because 'the less energy moral government has in society, the more indispensable it is for material government to gain in intensity, to prevent the entire decomposition of the social body' (1998: 199).

Comte's own individual intellectual and political position was not widely known in the 1820s and indeed his relative anonymity protected him on occasion from possible prosecution (Pickering, 1993: 133–8). His early writings only became Comtean (rather than Saint-Simonian) when they were republished in 1854. Comte only really became famous as a social thinker, as an intellectual in his own right, with the publication of the latter part of the *Course in Positive Philosophy* (that is the volumes of 1839–1842) and with his attempt to provide a general summation of his position in *A Discourse on the Positive Spirit* (published on its own in a small edition, and then included as an introduction to the *Traité Philosophique d'Astonomie Populaire* (1844)). In between these two works, Comte published a huge volume on geometry: the *Traité Élémentaire de Géométrie Analytique* (1843). These projects are all closely connected: science and theology are fundamentally opposed to each other, and it has been astronomy that has been the leading edge of the sciences in the struggle. The strategy here is political; it is to produce out of the scientific tradition and particularly the new arrival sociology, a new ethics. The new ethics will be organised by a new 'spiritual power' of educators and counsellors who now, he announces dramatically, will form an alliance with the newly emerging proletariat (see Kent, 1978: 69–83; Bensaude-Vincent, 1991; Pilbeam, 2000a: 172–235).

The 1844 Discourse presents again the law of the three states from the point of view of an introduction to a course on astronomy. The new aspects of which now appears as the following:

> The first of these states, though in every respect indispensable at the outset, must be regarded as purely provisional and preparatory. The second is but a modified and destructive form of the first, and thus has only the transitional function of leading gradually to the third. This last is the only normal and final state of human reason in all departments of knowledge.
>
> (Comte, 1903: 2)

The metaphysical state is 'a sort of distemper naturally supervening in … mental evolution' (1903: 17).

The antagonism between theological and positive methods is said to have existed throughout history, 'the principal, though not always discernible, source of the various transformations which have successively weakened the theological philosophy'. Thus:

> the metaphysical spirit … was never the true agent but only the instrument of dissolution. The positive spirit, by reason of the want of generality necessarily incident to its slow, piecemeal evolution, could not adequately formulate its own philosophical tendencies. Hence arose the special necessity for the intervention of the metaphysical spirit which alone could give something like a systematic shape to the spontaneous opposition of dawning science. (p. 57)

Comte presents another brief account of the European crisis over the last five centuries leading up to the 'great final crisis' (p. 80). Gradually the theological authorities were driven back into the church itself under the onslaught of metaphysical criticism. But when it came to the constructive moment of the revolution there was only a fatal disappointment and disillusion (p. 81). The rise of sciences introduces a modification in the structure of theological thought towards secularisation; but the metaphysical state is not able to function as a principal motor of historical development. This motor lies elsewhere.

The revolution in failing to complete the process merely inaugurated a period of oscillation between the retrogressive parties and the metaphysical party, neither of which was able to achieve a solution to the crisis. And then there appeared a 'stationary party', which tried to sanction both tendencies and to neutralise them. The result was again highly ambivalent. It had the consequence of creating a more stable situation, but only by 'erecting inconsistency into a system'.

> Far from tending to terminate the revolutionary crisis such an attitude could only have the effect of perpetuating it because it would be directly opposed to all true preponderance of any system … but it has its use if confined to the strictly temporary purpose of providing empirically for the most pressing difficulties of our revolutionary situation … the stationary system is at the present time not only inevitable but indispensable … The influence it has so rapidly acquired … shows more and more that the old convictions and passions … are dying out … and are being replaced with a real though confused feeling of the need and even the possibility of a permanent reconciliation between the spirit of conservation and the spirit of improvement. (p. 85)

The new condition is reluctantly welcomed as providing space for the working out of the positive doctrine while at least the government maintains at great cost a material order by force 'in the midst of intellectual disorder' (pp. 86–7).

A SOCIOLOGY OF THE 'METAPHYSICAL STATE'

In order to examine this, I will focus on what Comte called the 'intermediary' transitional state. It is clear that the conceptualisation of this state in Comte's work is always profoundly troubled. In the first formulation of the law of the three states, the second was defined as metaphysical and juridical, and 'its general character is that of possessing no well-defined characteristics'. It is not exceptional in being simply a phase of transition since the formation of the Catholic system was acknowledged to have taken ten centuries. This particular transitional state lies not between two forms of the theological stage (e.g. polytheism to monotheism), but is the whole transition between the two fundamental or 'normal' forms, theological and positive. It is the radical antagonism between these two basic forms, which explains for Comte, the virulence of the revolutionary crisis and why 'intermediary' metaphysical phenomena come into existence.

A number of new methodological reflections are important here. The first is that using the 'historical method' Comte's object is not a 'history' in the conventional sense itself but the abstracted history of a fictive being, that is, abstract 'Humanity'. The second is that Comte in dealing with the decline of one system and the rise of another locates the space for the analysis of these metaphysical phenomena from a sociological not historical point of view. The third is that the order of analysis is dependent on Comte's identification of the end states (the first, theological, and the third, positive) in order to define and identify the 'intermediary' state. Finally, Comte argues that knowledge of the future state, the positive state, is more certain than that of the present even though it too is fictive.

As well as these methodological points there is one very basic theoretical one to take into account. In his discussion of continuities and discontinuities in biology Comte argues that 'states do not evolve into each other by an internal logic', thus the displacement of one state by another is an externally driven one. In the transition in the West, the rise of the positive system induces the theological order to mutate towards metaphysics. The function of the metaphysical philosophy is to wage a purely negative and general critique of theology. Positive philosophy eventually creates the conditions that enable sociology to play a constructive and governing role in the life of the new society. What Comte works towards is a theory of the combination of states, and that revolutions are true reversals of an order of dominance within those combinations and structures of invariance. His problem is to show that the transition between theology and the social order to come is not simply one of the linear growth either of one of the major forces or indeed of the intermediate phenomena, since there is complexity and dominance. This problem is a pivotal one since Comte presents his orders of the 'twofold, or duplex movement' in relation to the end states. This mode of exposition gives the impression that the process of abstraction in the formation of the genealogies is in fact simply categorical, that is as simply a matter of arranging the known elements of the history into the prepared boxes, a naïve classification. But this cannot be the actual process here in Comte's analysis since he has three categories of facts but only two genealogical series. It is essential perhaps to make a general clarification here on a number of basic theoretical questions.

First, society as an organism exists in two different forms: either in the 'organic' form of a relatively stable social organism, or in a transitional form, an exceptional 'critical' form (this is Comte's solution to the problem raised by Bazard).

Second, since the fall of the Roman empire there has only been one social 'normal' organism in European history, the feudal-Catholic Middle-Ages, which have been followed by a state of exceptional transition, the *modern crisis*. Comte's messianic theory identifies the coming of a second organic transition. His analyses however are to be falsifiable demonstrations, even proof, of rational laws, not the revealed truths of a religious prophet. His aim is to introduce a new way of thinking about European history: the facts of this history are marshalled according to the intervention of a scientific conjecture. The wager here, as read in this perspective, is to introduce the law of the development of human knowledge, as the general law of the history of European society. In fact Comte pushes this further. It is not just a history of the individual mind, but all human social organisation is determined by this cognitive cultural logic either directly or indirectly.

My analysis here comes to the heart of the problem therefore. I suggest that the whole of the elaborate set of constructions in Comte's writings, the history of the sciences, the sociology, the positive philosophy and the utopia of the positive polity, are essentially the product of the tensions around a very precise difficulty: the necessity in Comte's thesis of a *radical discontinuity* between the metaphysical and the positive state. Thus it is from an appreciation of this difficulty that the functioning of the whole of Comte's project in the largest sense can be understood: that the crucial *continuity* in the modern transition is that of the rising positive series (which in Weberian terms is driven here by the force of rationalisation), and *not* from within (i.e. the fruits of deism) the crisis of the decomposition series.

This reading reveals why it is so important in Comte's view that European history is to be regarded as a combination of two irreconcilable

The decompositional series:
Catholicism → Protestantism → deism → [extinction of religion?]

The rising series:
physics → chemistry → biology → sociology → [a new kind of spiritual authority]

Figure 7.1 The crucial discontinuity in the modern crisis between deism (the decompositional series) and the positive polity (in the rising series) in CPP

systems, one declining and one rising: the key metaphysical elements and structures belong to the old order. These elements develop as modifications induced by the new underlying forces which are yet to complete their formation into a social organism. The argument hangs on the thesis that there is no crucial rupture between theology and metaphysics, the crucial break is not that between theological and post-theological modalities. The appearance of metaphysical phenomena is the sign of the formation of strong positivities in the system: they cannot and do not form a stable and viable social organism on their own. The theological and the positive states are 'organic' social organisms and without knowledge of these states the intermediary genealogies and Comte's periodisations cannot be known and identified (Gane, 2003: 18–23).

What is interesting and important here is Comte's presentation of his basic sociological law since there appears to be elements of a new interpretation. At the beginning of the 1844 Discourse he does not simply repeat the formulas found in the Course, here it is simplified: 'all our speculations on every subject of human inquiry are bound to pass successively, both in the individual and in the species, through three different theoretical states, usually known as theological, metaphysical, and positive' (1903: 2). By 1844 the conclusion is that the theological regime is truly over. The metaphysical regime is dominant in politics and morals; the positive state had triumphed in the main branches of industry and science.

The main driving force of development has been the positive movement, and more specifically it has been astronomy 'that has always hitherto been the chief motor ('moteur') in great intellectual revolutions' (1903: 171). He now stresses very simply that:

> before even assuming a truly scientific character, it was this class of conceptions that above all determined the decisive passage from fetishism to polytheism, everywhere issuing from the cult of the stars. Its first mathematical applications in the schools of Thales and Pythagoras were the principal intellectual source of the decay of polytheism and the rise of monotheism. Finally, the systematic rise of modern positivity … resulted in the great astronomical renewal begun by Copernicus, Kepler and Galileo. (1903: 169–70)

The birth of reason however emerges with the birth of humanity itself; the regularities of the world were experienced and recognised from the beginning. It is only the growth of the scientific, or more generally the positive spirit which exemplifies progression: in the spheres of theology and metaphysics there is change but it amounts merely to a fundamental repetition of attempts to answer questions that are 'radically insoluble' in onto-theological frameworks. The substance of the debates of the Greek philosophers was reproduced in new forms by the scholastic philosophers of the Middle Ages, and these were again reproduced in the schools of Condillac and Cousin. Metaphysical philosophy merely oscillates between restoring theology on the one hand, and outright negation on the other since it is incapable of generating anything new on its own account (p. 16). In the great intellectual crises metaphysical reflection always played an important part. Even in the transition from fetishism to polytheism, 'when purely supernatural activity was withdrawn from each particular body, and lodged in the gods' there was a process of metaphysical intellectual rationalisation, playing as Beesley expressed it 'an unconscious and imperceptible operation' (in Comte, 1903: xx).

It was in the transition from polytheism to monotheism that the spirit of a metaphysical ontology really came fully into the open. It remained under the dominance of theology until that regime too finally began to decay. After that, the role of metaphysics began to play an ambivalent role and to hinder the development of science. In the end it became the 'most dangerous obstacle' to progress (1903: 19). But the way in which the positive movement had effects in philosophy and politics gave rise to some interesting parallels: in the Middle Ages there was a compromise philosophy of the scholastics which argued that it was God who had established natural laws that he 'had forbidden himself ever to change'. Constitutional monarchy is another example where 'the political type is in fact based on reasons furnished by the theological type' (p. 61–2). This observation matches Comte's view that the sovereignty of the people is a structural inversion of the principle of the divine right of kings.

The account of the radical incompatibility or antagonism of science and theology is stark and sombre in these pages (pp. 53–64). To correct any misunderstanding he returns to the formula of the law of the three states given in his opening sections of the 1844 Discourse, where he implied that the dissolution of theology was the work of metaphysics (p. 57). In fact before the rise of a systematic positive philosophy to organise the scientific movement, this role was taken by metaphysicians, based on the work of astronomy. Pushing his argument he suggests that Greek polytheism was in the last analysis 'incompatible with the foundation of mathematical astronomy' (p. 58). If science flourished to a greater degree under monotheism, it was because it did not have to struggle 'at each separate step, against the dangerous rivalry of a specific supernatural explanation' (p. 59), eventually this brought the two systems, theology and science, into direct conflict. One or the other will triumph:

> For as long as there is any theological belief at all, even of the most attenuated kind, there must always be the lurking thought, even though it may not take definite shape, that the order of nature is liable to sudden and arbitrary disturbance. Indeed were not for this obstacle – which nothing but the entire extinction of the theological spirit can remove – the daily spectacle of the really existing order would long ago have caused the cardinal principle of the positive philosophy (the invariability of natural laws) to be universally accepted. (1903: 60)

This statement of theory is also a declaration of war.

The Discourse of 1844 also proclaims a programme of universal education, and full employment aimed principally at the working classes. It is interesting to note that Comte gave free lecture courses on astronomy in the Third Arrondissement in Paris for many years (1830–1847). At their most popular, the lectures, lasting some three hours, were attended by as many as 400 people (in 1843). Encyclopaedic education is the issue that is dealt with at length. In the 1844 Discourse he announced that positivism will reconstruct modern culture as a whole (p. 43):

> The positive spirit therefore must be the one determining principle of that great intellectual communion upon which all true human association must rest, though it has to be coupled with two other fundamental conditions – a sufficient conformity of feeling, and some convergence of interests.

He continues: 'There is no longer any true community of opinion in Europe except as to those branches of knowledge in which the positive method already prevails.' It would be possible to show, he says:

> that the positive philosophy alone is capable of gradually realizing that noble project of universal association which Catholicism prematurely tried to build up in the Middle Ages. That attempt failed because the Catholic philosophy … had insufficient logical coherence to enable it to accomplish this social aim. (pp. 40–1)

The 1844 text is certainly a manifesto, a manifesto that declares the positive spirit to be the radical enemy of theology. Its declared aim is to discredit theology on methodological grounds: the positive spirit does not attempt to answer insoluble problems. The doctrines of theology have been ejected from science in discipline after discipline, and the method of revelation or divination have been shown to be radically incompatible with science. The new spiritual power will establish itself on the basis of a new kind of authority – in relation to temporal powers that again will be legitimated on the grounds of competence, of capacity. He goes on to say that 'positive conceptions are incompatible with theological opinions of any kind, monotheistic no less than polytheistic or fetishistic' (p. 53), a formula which came to be an embarrassment only four years later. The text itself works towards an expression which also came later to be something of an embarrassment. He says that the positive movement is 'not compatible with religious preoccupations' (1903: 51). Beesley, provided a critical note at this point to say that 'by religion here he means theology'.

8

Spiritual Power, Sociology and Humanity

In the Preface (1851) to the first volume of the System, Comte refers to a letter of 2nd June 1845, as indicating the nature of his 'regenerated' moral state (it is given in SPP, appendix, pp. 613–18); and the first effects were worked out in his public lecture course of 1847, and then in his book *Discours Sur l'Ensemble du Positivisme* (translated as 'The General View of Positivism') in 1848. This 1848 Discourse became, with additions, the first of the four volume *System of Positive Polity* published between 1851–4. The full title of the System was *Système de Politique Positive, ou Traité du Sociologie Instituant La Religion de l'Humanité.* 1856 saw the first of an uncompleted four volume project, called the Subjective Synthesis. And supplementing these texts he also published two book length popularisations *Catéchisme Positiviste* (1852), and his *Appel aux Conservateurs* (1855). This set of substantial volumes published between 1848 and 1856 adds a whole new layer of analysis, on affect, emotion, and gender relations, to the law of the three states which is completely reorganised: 'Every man, in the successive periods of his life, differs from himself no less than at any one time he differs from others' he said (cited by Vernon, 1986: 282). In this reconstructed position Comte openly attempted to fuse together his personal and his intellectual life. At the beginning of the System, he wrote, 'The primary object of positivism is twofold, to generalise our scientific conceptions, and to systematise the art of social life' (SPP, I, 2). How did he come to take this immense change of direction, from a project to establish a new universal association, to one of establishing a new universal religion?

Certainly Comte himself claimed continuity, since he had referred previously to the new association as a 'church' (1975, II, 696) or hinted that the attempt would surpass the Catholic Church of the Middle Ages (the 1844 Discourse, Comte: 1903, 43). The question of the coherence of these ideas arises perhaps because of terminological ambiguity or some misunderstanding of theory, since the reader of Comte is certainly familiar with the thesis that the positive movement is hostile to all religion, theology and metaphysics, to which it finds itself in radical opposition. Is this a problem of terminology perhaps, because technically Comte's objections are to theology and metaphysics as methods and the concept he wishes to develop in a broader sense is 'religion'? The problem arises because he has himself often embraced the opposition between religion and science as identical in meaning to the distinction between theology and science. The shift in meaning and scope of the term 'religion' is thus crucial. Before looking at the key text, the 1848 Discourse, it is important to look at the contextual changes taking place in France at this juncture.

THE CHANGING FRENCH CONTEXT

When examined closely there are some evident difficulties in assessing the so-called 'madness' of the later Comte. In referring to the 'lunacy' of the idea of establishing a religion with oneself as its High Priest or Pope commentators fail to recognise that Comte was not the only one to attempt this in France in the first part of the nineteenth century. Judging Comte against a laicised France where education and the state are maintained as a religion-free zone, and where for the most part political organisations are secular, can only lead to misunderstandings and misinterpretation. It was Engels for example in reporting the state of socialism and communism in Europe in 1843 who found it strange and indeed 'curious' that while in England these movements tended to be non-religious even anti-religious, in France 'being a part of a nation celebrated for its infidelity' they 'are themselves Christians. One of their favorite axioms is, that Christianity *is* Communism' (in Marx and Engels, 1975: 399). After the revolutionary period and the Napoleonic empire, there was a considerable religious revival. Yet this took place in a particular way. Weakened by the ravages of the revolution, the Catholic Church itself found itself very short of personnel (in 1828 there were 5,000 church vacancies), and in many parts of France the mass could not be celebrated. At the same time from 1816, Christianity was required in primary schools, and from 1833 with a law introduced by Guizot, each school was obliged to have a crucifix or image of Jesus in its classrooms. The revival in the church was led by priests newly recruited from rural areas, and new ranks of *instituteurs* in the classroom brought in virtually untrained recruits. The revival was accompanied by 'an explosion of religious theorizing, christocentric in orientation but at odds with official Catholic doctrine' (Berenson, 1989: 553).

Engels noted that such was the degree of repression in France if it were asked 'why do not the French communists establish communities, as the English have done? My reply would be, because they *dare* not. If they did, the first experiment would be put down by soldiers' (in Marx and Engels, 1975: 398). There were many attempts at insurrection during these years. They were all put down by force. A shift to other oppositional methods was evident. One was, following Saint-Simon's last work, attempts at organising a 'new Christianity', and in reaction, other attempts such as that by Cabet, to develop a 'true Christianity' (Pilbeam, 2000b: 499). The shift towards religion involved not a return to the theocratic eighteenth-century religion of fear, but to a religion of love, fraternity, and moral regeneration from below: 'virtually everyone who considered himself a socialist claimed to be inspired by Christianity. The Gospels were everywhere' (Berenson, 1989: 543). Alphonse Esquiros was imprisoned for publishing his *L'Evangile du Peuple* of 1840. Louis Blanc published a *Catéchisme Socialiste* with Jesus as hero. Across the spectrum from the neo-Catholics to the socialists the emphasis was on fraternity, submission and obedience not liberty. Lamennais, the leading social Catholic, interpreted fraternity to mean obedience to a regime of equality against the 'reign of Satan' of those who occupied elite positions of power. Cabet's movement too envisaged a humanity delivered from satan. The Catholic literature of the love of Jesus, like the *Imitation of Christ* by Thomas à Kempis became widely popular. The theme of non-violence and love predominated, and in 1844 Pecqueur wrote that 'true religion consists in the practice of the law of fraternity, which is to say in the love of humanity through the love of God' (cited in Berenson, 1989: 556). Victor Considérant wrote: 'Destinies are the present, past and future plans established by God, in conformity with the laws of mathematics' (cited in Pilbeam, 2000b: 505).

There were a number of experimental religions on the margins of Catholicism itself, some of which were closed by the state. There was the Eglise Chrétienne Primitive, the Eglise Constitutionnelle Française (closed in 1832), and the Eglise Catholique Française. The Abbé Châtel, who ordained priests, produced a Code de l'Humanité that denied the Trinity, sin and the holy virgin; he was banned from practicing by the state. Louis de Tourreil announced 1845 as Year One of a new epoch of his new religion of Fusionisme in which God fused male, female and love into 'Mèramourpère' inhabiting a universe in which the stars were alive. He specified rituals and prayers in detail, and symbolic gestures that replaced the Catholic sign of the cross (see Charlton, 1963: 132–3). Ganneau in a parallel mission taught that redemption was to come through women, and that God was the people (see Starkie, 1954: 50–5, 205–8). Clearly the Saint-Simonian religion in 1828 with its emphasis on love, its organised hierarchies and rituals, its doctrine of the spiritual power of the two popes (male and female), its missions, was an early highly energetic and intense precursor to this significant effervescence: 'In the absence of the official Church, French men and women had, by 1830, become accustomed to practising religion as they wanted it to be' (Berenson, 1989: 551). Comte had maintained a distance both from Saint-Simon's 'new Christianity', the religion of the 'Saint-Simonians' and all the religious sects around it like that of Buchez, and from the social Catholics like Lammenais. He produced a coherent critique of Christianity as based on a purely egoistic ethics, and a withering critique of the Christocentric doctrine. Nevertheless the idea of a spiritual power had been expressed briefly as a new church, a new universal association to match and surpass medieval Catholicism.

In 1840s he lost a substantial part of his income from examining at the Ecole Polytechique, and the rest in 1851. Never wealthy he now faced impoverishment. He was for a time supported by funds donated by his supporters in England and France. After the publication of the Discourse of (February) 1844, aged forty-six, 'short, pot-bellied, and balding' (Pickering, 2000) he had met, in April, and fallen in love with the sister of one of his pupils, Clotilde de Vaux, a young aspiring writer aged thirty, who had been abandoned by her husband. Tragically, she was to die – of tuberculosis – in his presence only twelve months later. His relation with her was characterised by his attempt to convince her of the grandeur and importance of his intellectual system, and by her attempts to retain her distance from him and his system (Pickering, who reads their relationship as 'an intense battle', 2000: 141). The two women in his life, Caroline Massin and Clotilde de Vaux did not in reality fit the submissive, feminine, non-intellectual stereotype he pronounced he was seeking. His ideas on love were also evidently at odds with the prevailing religious debates which were Christocentric and humanistic, as his critique of the importance of Jesus to Christianity and ethics more generally was to reveal in detail. Although only as far back as 1844 he had argued fetishism was completely incompatible with positivist ideas, the religious practices he now began to embrace involved fetishistic elements. He worshipped the objects Clotilde was associated with, the chair she sat on when visiting him, and a lock of her hair. A rumour, untrue, circulated by a rival cult claimed that after her death he had cut off her hand and worshipped it (Pickering, 1998: 76).

After April 1846 he interpreted the strong emotional effect on him of this platonic relationship as one of religious regeneration and discipline, making possible his own construction the Religion of Humanity as a religion of love, with its own hierarchical order, discipline and iconolatry. These included detailed positive prayers (modelled on his adoration of Clotilde, a subjective mathematics and symbolic gestures which replace the sign of the cross (they indicated the principal organs of the body). His plans to become the High Priest of the new religion specify that his authority, and income, would eventually be considerable and as soon as the religion got under way his financial worries seemed to be relieved. Many have drawn the conclusion that there was madness here. In context, this view has to be doubted. His new situation is a solution to all of his problems in one fell sweep: personal, political, financial, theoretical. He becomes the first sociocratic priest in a new religious movement devoted to love and to the worship of Humanity, with late Clotilde as icon. It solves his financial problems. If he lost his rationalist colleagues, particularly Littré and Mill, on the one hand, he gained new acolytes who rapidly began to spread the new message throughout the world, on the other. His ideas for a new spiritual power in Europe, previously disseminated through his scientific and political writings were now also to be disseminated in a religious idiom. This was not the explosive, volcanic form of proselytism of the Saint-Simonians (with its carnal 'rehabilitation of the flesh'), but a cool, studied, puritanical new repression of the flesh (Wernick, 2001: 124–35).

From the mid-1840s, then, Comte began an auto-critique. His previous positions, he reflected, did not sufficiently mark itself off from a major weakness of modernity, the revolt of reason against the emotions leading to the overdevelopment of reason against the heart. If the emotions were important what had been the consequences of omitting them from his system? What had been the consequences of concentrating too much on the role of the intellect in the law of the three states? He made new and important connections between religion, love and the emotions, and the relations more generally concerning the importance of women in social evolution. He saw a whole new dimension of philosophy and sociology open up, and his new perspectives were directly drawn from his personal experiences which he now began to recount in his writings. He intensified his practices of cerebral hygiene. Merging the personal and the sociological, the public and private, in ways which remain controversial, he proclaimed that he was 'living openly'. He transformed his purely philosophical view that modernity involved an abnormal revolt of the present against the past into a cult based around the worship of the most worthy and loved past representatives of Humanity on the model of the Catholic commemoration of the saints. From the moment of Clotilde's death Comte's work began to be marked by a generalised ambiance of mourning and melancholy and a revalorisation of the dead, in fact a 'religion of the living dead' (Braunstein, 2003). This was to be a religion without a theology, and he proclaimed himself as its first hierophant. He was living in a new way: 'posthumously'. Indeed he quickly assumed the position as the pope in the new positive church and began to issue papal instructions, *brefs* (Littré, 1879). His earlier contempt for parodies of Catholicism was forgotten as it seemed that out of Saint-Simonianism there was to be yet another turn to religiosity, another sacred college. To Mill and Littré, and those who wanted to continue the work of rationalist sociology, this turn appeared as both theoretically retrogressive and when Comte accepted and appealed – after 1852 – for support from Napoleon III, politically reactionary, a complete betrayal. Nevertheless, rashly, Comte announced in 1854 – counting, wrongly as it turned out, on the adoption of his new religion by Napoleon's nephew, that the definitive era of the third state, the positive polity, would begin definitively in 1856. The new orientations seemed to imply huge shifts in political position and allegiances. And the political break was eventually manifested at length in his *Appeal to Conservatives* ([1855] 1889). His move to the puritanical right was just as radical in his proposal for an ultra-puritanical reorganisation of gender relations.

COMTE'S ALIENATION FROM THE TRADITIONAL AND THE NEW PATRIARCHICAL SYSTEMS

As has been pointed out this is a new aspect in Comte's thought, a version of 'feminine authority ... diffused throughout the society's domestic life' which is linked to a recognition that 'the place of women is one of central importance, for it is only through the domestic influence of wives and mothers that the religion of humanity, in most cases, achieves acceptance' (Vernon, 1986: 278). Here Comte's aim is to reverse the tendency to the debasement of love in Western culture, and to oppose the new Saint-Simonian feminism and the demand for equality between the sexes reflected in Enfantin's call for the female messiah (Moses, 1982). Comte poses this issue again historically as a problem of the loss of the ideals of chivalry and courtly love of the medieval period (and ties it to a revised phrenological analysis (Wernick, 2001: 125–49)). The aim of his neopatriarchalism is to restore some substance to the idealisation and purification which the medieval practice seems to inspire, otherwise he argues modern morality will fall below the standard of the Middle Ages and sink into a new sexual anarchy. He commends the principle of eternal widowhood (with certain limited exceptions which would have applied to Clotilde), and reasserts the value of the social segregation of the sexes. The woman should obey the husband, but the latter should adopt the cult of woman and guardian angels. Whereas Enfantin suggested that paternity be the mother's secret and the state the institution to superintend socialisation of all children, Comte's radical hypothesis is that all sexual relations in society should be replaced by a utopia of virgin motherhood a utopia which will itself improve the status of women. The utopia would give virgin mothers complete control of human reproduction and socialisation; men would form a patriarchal union of brothers and 'fathers', whose authority would remain in a milieu which would 'make women feel the merit of submission, by drawing out to its consequences this admirable maxim of Aristotle: the greatest strength of woman lies in overcoming the difficulty of obeying' (Comte, 1891a: 228). The new sociology provides scientific justification for submission.

The specific idioms of the purifying cult of woman were developed, theorised and practised in the organised forms of the new 'religion': the nature of the image of women, the prayers, the language, the gestures (Comte, 1907). The objective is moral purification and social and personal mental hygiene. What women will do precisely is left as an open question to be developed and solved by women themselves – an echo of Enfantin *appel de la femme*. Through the segregated and hierarchical structures, through idealisation and duty, a new stability can be attained. The programme for the family is intended to end the state of conflict within the domestic sphere – a metaphysical stage epitomised by the rise of feminist thought. Once the final stage is achieved, the progressive development of science itself comes to an end in a stable system of harmonised known laws which are all made conscious of their place in the totality by the new priesthood. It seems from that point, social life will be made up of rituals, ceremonials, reenactments, in a word theatricalisations, of the various aspects of the three state law. In this sense the law seems to reflect Comte's own deep longing that the pain of modernity be ended so that everything will have found its rightful place. Comte noted in 1852 that it is feeling which is 'the sole existing preservative of Western society from a complete and irreparable dissolution. Since the close of the Middle Ages, the influence of women has been the sole though unacknowledged check on the moral evils attaching to the mental alienation towards which the West more and more tended to, especially its centre – France'. He insisted that it is only when men begin to think under 'the inspiration of woman' can they 'bring synthesis into constant harmony with sympathy' (Kofman, 1978: 159–71).

Comte initiated a particular type of combination of psychology and sociology; he accepted phrenology was the most adequate representation of scientific psychology, although he recognised it was still at an early stage of development. In a sense this immaturity suited his purposes in a number of ways, and he tried to work out a system of phrenology which would overcome common objections. Indeed this active kind of intervention was one of the goals of positive philosophy in its attempt to show that sciences benefited from mutual review and adjustment of method and content. His phrenology therefore came more and more to mirror the needs of his sociology and his Religion of Humanity. It is not surprising that his understanding of the relations between the genders reflected fundamental divisions in the different types of brains of men and women, and verified in phrenological investigation. Comte connects this point in a simple and direct fashion with reproductive function and anatomy (reflected in the different locations of sexual and maternal instincts) and drew the conclusion from his analysis that it is woman who has the 'highest type of the mutual influence of the cerebral and the bodily life.' This has been made possible in social development by the fact that she has been 'set free from the pressure of active life, and made more and more amenable to the influence of the emotions, especially of the sympathetic emotions' (Wernick 2001: 142f.). The Comtean system here begins to furnish a complete and harmonised neo-patriarchal system: woman is to remain separated from active life, in order to develop the highest form of physical and moral unity. The power of women, like the power of the priesthood is exercised hegemonically.

THE SPIRITUAL POWER AND POST-HUMANIST RELIGION

It is clear that Comte had, from his earliest considerations back in 1817, talked and speculated about the need for new spiritual corporations and what their functions would be. At the end of the Course in 1842, he even referred to its future as a 'church'. He had referred to the renewal of the priesthood and papacy of the Middle Ages as a new kind of spiritual power that could be taken as a model. But, given Comte's consistent criticism even ridicule of any writer who thought that this could be achieved literally; no one was really prepared for what Comte now proposed. The radical intellectuals around Comte were at first quite silent, and then were quick to take up their positions. On the one hand Comte was optimistic that one of the temporal powers would adopt and promote the new religion (he wrote many appeals, some of which were spectacularly maladroit), but failing that option as soon as he began to attract a different kind of adherent. Excluded from the university sphere, he began to build the new priesthood himself from scratch.

Against expectations throughout this period the central problems of his sociology were still being worked through. The law of the three states was continuously under review and revision as it became the basis of a religion. Previously the law had combined intellectual and practical 'couples' – Catholic-feudalism, scientific-industrialism. He now added the emotions as an affective dimension, and so doing brought for the first time into sociology the issues of gender and more specifically the analysis of the position of women in the social system. In his encounter with Clotilde he had been asked the question: where and what is the place of love for positive social science? Comte admitted his system suffered from intellectual dryness. Not only did he need a sociology of the emotions, he needed a rationale for his sociology in terms of the emotions. If he answered these questions by reconstructing his system in terms of a 'religion of love' what he meant by 'love' was not the current Christocentric form; it was a combination of chivalric idealisation, mystic worship in the mode of Thomas à Kempis, and fetishistic adoration. Given Comte's immense inventiveness he added to the list of words he had coined, positivism, and sociology, a new concept for this orientation governing the ethics of his new religion of love: altruism (SPP, I, 502).

The decompositional series:
Catholicism⟶Protestantism⟶deism⟶[atheism/civic humanism?]

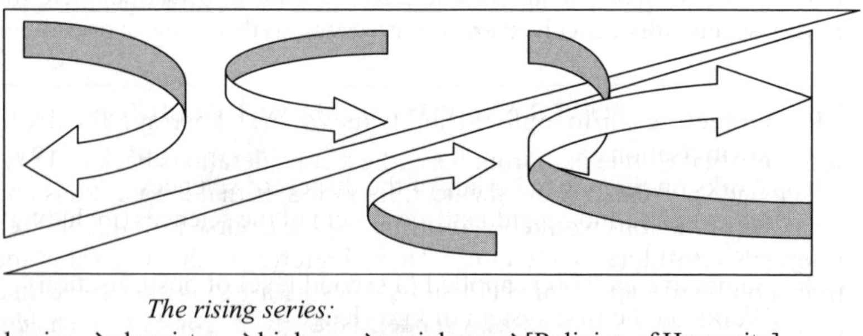

The rising series:
physics⟶chemistry⟶biology⟶sociology⟶[Religion of Humanity]

Figure 8.1 The crucial discontinuity in the modern crisis between post-deism (the decompositional series) and the Religion of Humanity (in the rising series) in SPP

In the Course (1842), he had intended he said to inaugurate a practice of harmonising, adjusting, regulating the entire system of objective knowledge, and then founding the new science of sociology as the sixth science. In the System of Positive Polity, he was to attempt, he said, to harmonise the whole of human knowledge from a subjective, a religious point of view, and to found a seventh science, a new ethics based on extreme altruism. We might represent this trajectory from the Course to the System in Figure 8.2.

The completed System is therefore something which might be said to involve a two-fold hermeneutic. The objective method in philosophy works on the spontaneous development of the sciences to harmonise and govern them in a first hermeneutic, a first reading (in fact there is an ambiguity in the Course about the precise nature of the discussion of sociology which Comte attempts to clear up in its final three lectures, 57–60). The analysis using the subjective method is a second order philosophical discourse which goes beyond harmonisation as such. It frees itself from the limits posed by scientific objectivity and transforms the new system of sciences into an ethics, the basis of the teachings organised by a new spiritual authority. The apparatus seems remarkably similar to what Latour has called a regime of 'factishes' (Latour, 1999: 275); Latour says: 'Like Comte I believe sociology is the Queen of the sciences … exactly important as Comte imagined […] of course he was a complete madman … but the idea he had of sociology being a master of ceremonies of the collective (to use my term) was right' (in Gane, 2004: 89).

The first operation opens up the possibility of a new corporation of scientists whose function and organisation is largely devoted to education (Comte begins to outline its precise organisation). The second operation is very specifically conceived as having a religious discipline, a priesthood

I	Objective philosophical analysis (a first abstract level of positivisation) Works on the raw materials of the dispersed sciences To complete and co-ordinate the system of the sciences (including sociology).
II	Subjective method is applied (a second level of positivisation) Works on the first system of knowledge To complete the system of ethics, found the new Religion of Humanity (altruism), in combination with I.

Figure 8.2 Comte's double hermeneutic

that aims to attain a purely intellectual and moral hegemony over the temporal powers. The whole formation is the positive polity.

THE NEW SUBJECTIVE METHODOLOGY

The question to be examined here is what Comte meant by the 'subjective method'. The shifts in his work are clearly registered and the linkage between his personal, private life and his public life became more systematic. At the beginning of the System, he asks the reader to note the differences between the Prefaces to the two major works (Course and System). In the first, it is intellect and objectivity that play the main role. In the second it is 'feeling' and subjectivity. He says: 'When … I passed in 1836 from Cosmology to Biology, I at once saw that the exclusion on scientific grounds of the subjective method could only be provisional … my first chapter on biology showed a glimpse of the final harmony between the two logics' (SPP, I, xii). The first operations in the objective mode attempt to complete an 'encyclopaedic unity', the second operations in the subjective mode attempt to complete a new 'synthesis' which embraces 'the whole order of the world' from the point of view of Humanity.

From 1848, Comte presents the introduction of the subjective method as following a new order of priorities; from now on in his work the 'heart guides and rules the intellect which will henceforth serve it' (SPP, I, 12). Since his earlier ideas about social evolution held that the driving force of social progression was intellectual enlightenment, he now dramatically questions its purity and primacy. He writes, characteristically pushing his argument to extremes, that:

> so feeble is our intellect that the impulse of some sort of passion is necessary to direct and sustain it in almost every effort. When the impulse [to discover truths] comes from kindly feelings it attracts attention on account of its rarity or value; when it springs from the selfish motives of glory, ambition, or gain, it is too common to be remarked … It does indeed occasionally happen that the intellect is actuated by a sort of passion for truth itself, without any mixture of pride of vanity. Yet in this case, as in every other, there is intense egotism in exercising the mental powers irrespectively of all social objects. Positivism as I shall afterwards explain, is even more severe than Catholicism in its condemnation of this type of character, whether in metaphysicians or in men of science.
>
> (SPP, I, 13)

There is, emerging here, an ethic of extreme self-abnegation, not simply as an ethical ideal but as the recognition of the real nature of intellectual endeavour and the pursuit of scientific truth. The process of rationalisation is not driven by Reason (in fact Comte regards this as a metaphysical illusion), it is driven by ulterior motives, egotism, gain, glory, pride, vanity, etc., or love. What interests him is a search for an ethic of intellectual work and industry which is entirely devoted to a higher service (troubadours (see Serres, 1997), Gay Science (Nietzsche) all inspired by these ideas), for post-theological, post-metaphysical – that is post-human – values, for the cult of Humanity is not a humanism, and does not arise out of a 'humanist' tradition with its image of the integral human actor and personality with subjective depth.

The first and principal change in position is therefore emphasis on the fact that the intellect no longer rules. It is placed in the service of the theological and metaphysical polities and their emphasis on egoism, self-interest, and personal gain, or placed in the service of Humanity itself. In fact this becomes one aspect of his definition of the new polity, with the proviso that the intellect must not be humiliated or placed in any condition of 'abject submission' for this would inevitably provoke rebellion (p. 14). Second, the subjective method nevertheless has to recognise that it will work not on the evidence of the world and society directly, but from the knowledge produced by the system of the scientific disciplines. Comte is completely aware of this paradox arising from the twofold hermeneutic. The subjective principle is primary, but it can only be effective if it relates to the world discovered and organised by science. The very source of the moral unity of Humanity is external to it. It comes from the outside existing 'independently of us in the external world. That basis consists for us in the laws of order of the phenomena by which Humanity is regulated … as soon as the intellect has enabled us to comprehend it, it becomes possible for the feeling of love to exercise a controlling influence over our discordant tendencies' (SpP, I, 17).

This problem seems to be of the same order as that faced by Comte when he tried to establish sociology as a science: at the same time to found it and to place it and harmonise it in a system of sciences. In this case the question concerns the problem: how to attain an objective knowledge of Humanity of which that knowledge must itself be the servant? He begins to question the relationship between egoism and what he calls 'the social instincts' – in fact, the new term he coined to facilitate this analysis, altruism, does not appear in the 1848 Discourse. It appears in the first volume of System in a chapter on biology published in 1851 (SPP, I, 500). How is it, fundamentally, that egoism is not completely predominant and exclusive? Where are the natural springs of the social sympathies? The new Religion of Humanity seeks to displace the dominance of egoism with new social sympathies in a cult that is driven by motives that are higher than those of any previous religion. In these pages Comte outlines a general set of ideas about the natural world and a concept reviled up until now in his writings, stigmatised previously as irredeemably metaphysical. The fundamental thesis is that nature should not be thought of as a perfect system, but as replete with radical imperfections. It is not an untouchable sacrosanct totality, but one that is in many ways capable of being modified to the benefit of Humanity. Scientific study is not undertaken only for its own sake in the new context; it is expressly undertaken out of a love for Humanity. It is thus not fatalistic here, nor materialistic: it must exercise hegemony and not take power. Its aim is to establish a moral order with sufficient moral authority to overrule government, for it must 'never be permitted to govern' directly in its own right (p. 289).

In the 1848 Discourse, he does not give any further specification of what he means by the subjective method. But in the chapters added to the 1848 text that form the first sections of volume one of the System in 1851 he begins to round out his conception in more detail. Following on a discussion of Kant's analysis of the relation between observer and phenomena the text works towards a consideration that must trouble any lingering adherents to the Course. Here his new philosophy and theory alters the priorities and so begins to challenge views which place great importance on its accounts of historical development on the clash of methodologies, the principle of the radical antagonism of the three methods, and indeed the explanation of the crisis of Humanity on the basis of the conflict of the three methods. He says simply and as it turns out misleadingly, that with the Religion of Humanity, the period of the antagonism between the methods is at an end. He says 'the provisional exclusion of the subjective method' from the positive sciences is over. The two methods will be from now on 'mutually adjusted' to each other as both are subject to 'systematic revision' (p. 361). Given the significance of this revolution, it is somewhat surprising to say the least that Comte does not make more of it.

There is a proviso, and any reader expecting here a complete rapprochement of science with theology will be surprised and disappointed. But at least Comte's conception of the subjective method is clarified. The end of the war of the methodologies, he says, will only be accomplished on one very important condition, that the subjective method 'no longer' be dedicated to the search for hidden causes but be used only in the search for laws to ameliorate human nature and human circumstances (pp. 361–2). It 'must become sociological' (p. 362). On these conditions the two methods will enter into a 'natural harmony' constituting a new logic. There will be no fusion of methods into a single methodological synthesis, nor an eclectic reconciliation (as with Victor Cousin's philosophy). The synthesis is the result of combining the methods in a certain way. Comte describes the new relationship:

> The long antagonism of analysis and synthesis passes into a permanent alliance, in which each method will in its own way supplement the principal shortcomings of the other. The objective method used alone is of great value, when wisely employed … Conversely, the subjective method exclusively employed, while keeping the system as a whole constantly before us, would not leave the mind sufficiently free to gather the materials necessary for the stability of the edifice. It is only by a skilful combination of these two methods used alternatively, the one beginning where the other leaves off, that the defectiveness of each can be remedied; and thus the best use made of our small supply of intellectual force, so inadequate when left to itself for the social problems with which it has to deal. No doctrine of the final religion can be considered as satisfactorily established until it has passed through the ordeal of both methods.
>
> (SPP, I, 364)

It is important to recognise that what Comte is really saying is that the alignments in the methodological warfare have changed. Theology and metaphysics are now aligned against a new 'coupling': fetishism and positivism.

THE IMPLICATIONS OF THE NEW METHODOLOGY

There are more surprises to come in Comte's second volume published in 1852. Here he provides an account of the evolution of the subjective method which embraces all those methods prior to the formation of the positive sciences. Emerging in this analysis is Comte's new judgement that the earliest methods, those of fetishism, are now judged far superior to those of what he now calls 'theologism' (which include polytheism, monotheism, and, in effect, metaphysics). Although theologism establishes the institution of the priesthood, it was fetishism that recognised the power of moral regulation in personal life, and even as a general order of knowledge was superior to theologism (SPP, II, 75). In the third volume of 1853 it becomes very clear that the subjective method is finally identified by Comte as the fetishistic method itself. This may come as a surprise but that is because he says 'modern thinkers … simply do not place themselves at the proper point of view' (SPP, III, 77).

Comte reviews previous attempts to achieve a general synthesis. The Greeks' attempts at synthesis by using metaphysics were unsuccessful (SPP, III, 279). Perhaps it is now also surprising to read his new analysis of the mediaeval period itself. He argues that it was not at all the doctrines of Christianity which is important in this pivotal period of monotheism, which up to now has formed the basis of his social theory of European evolution: as the Christian doctrine became more systematically integrated the more it became incapable of developing a genuine intellectual and moral synthesis. His new estimation, bluntly expressed, recognises 'the total incapacity of the method based on causes to effect the coordination of society' (SPP, III, 354). The new orientation of Comte's thinking concludes:

> Of the three successive phases of the absolute philosophy [i.e. 'theologism' – MG] fetishism alone kept the emotional life directly in view. Polytheism was more favourable to the intellectual and practical sides of our nature. But this was more due to the instinctive efforts of its founders than to the character of the doctrine itself; and it was, moreover, effected at the sacrifice of feeling. Monotheism, it is true, seemed in the West to restore the heart to its proper position. But this was the result of external influences; for in the East, where the situation was different, we find Monotheism sanctioning the warlike life. Neither of these results had any relation to the doctrine in question. They are simple consequences of the social environment, which in the one case tended to encourage, in the other to obliterate, the distinction between the temporal and the spiritual power.
>
> (SPP, III, 354–5)

So the importance of the Catholic moment in this assessment was due not in fact to a result of its status as a special kind of intellectual method at all. He concludes not only was it 'the wisdom of the priesthood and the influence of the situation naturally and concurrently reacting upon it' (SPP, III, 355) that brought about the Catholic advance. It was a situation in which the 'wisdom of the priesthood' operated in contradiction to Christian doctrine itself: 'it seconded the spontaneous energy of the sympathetic instincts, although the Christian creed denied their very existence … none of these compensations could have been foreseen by Roman statesmen, who could not but be shocked by the anti-social tone of the new opinions' (SPP, III, 349). Now Rome is seen as the higher more complete formation.

The discussion of the subjective method leads Comte towards a reconsideration of the interrelations of intellect, action and what he variously calls feeling, emotion, morals, affect. To locate and explain this domain he draws freely on his own version of phrenology, and his own recent personal experiences. The model of worship and prayer, and the model story of moral regeneration through fetishistic love guided by science turns out to be his own story. And this produces several new consequences for the law of the three states. Where are the sources of such moral generation in the legacy of Humanity itself? The answer is that they are like the sciences to be found outside the theological tradition. The implication at this stage is that if they are outside this tradition they must either be linked in some way to another tradition, or be completely free floating. It seems clear that he thinks both fetishism and positivism are naturally aligned in a situation in which natural submission, adoration and veneration, altruism, are predominant. Individualism and egoism rise into prominence and predominance with the emergence of polytheism and monotheism and reaches its height with the theories of the sovereignty of the individual self and doctrines of the untrammelled individualism of the metaphysical polity. He himself, out of his own experiences, will provide the new materials for the new religion.

9

A Second Sociology

Comte turns strategically to the questions concerning the role of the subjective method: is it outside scientific sociology, or is it in some sense always required in sociological construction?

The crucial issue concerns the way in which the terms are posed and defined. In the way the sociological theses are presented, we are confronted with a problem of analysing the production and organisation of knowledge. In fact these are two linked but different activities. In Comte's theory it is a characteristic of the subjective method that final and absolute causal explanations dominate. Comte is radically relativist. It enables him to pose the problem of the relative consistency of scientific knowledge and to identify a role for philosophy in harmonising knowledge into a single system. The fact that in this order of thinking there is no appeal to an inaccessible level of ultimate causation, means that objective knowledge is produced within a frame of verifiable and falsifiable propositions. The practice of organising already produced objective knowledge from the point of view of Humanity can be seen to be a possible function for a subjectively based mode of synthesis and synergy. This is a basic function of a new kind of philosophy: organising knowledge. Absolute and relative modes of thought are brought together from now on in form which aims to neutralise their radical heterogeneity.

But there is a deeper relation of philosophy to science even within that of the production of knowledge itself according to Comte. This results from the fact that science does not simply identify things. In the objective method, it classifies them; it searches for necessary relations; it attempts to explain them concretely and abstractly. Science is not established in the move from a random databank (if such a thing is possible) to a systematic empiricism, but is constituted in a set of theoretical and empirical disjunctions and conjunctions between theory and evidence. This means that within scientific activity itself there is an order of reflection, conception, theory, speculation, idealisation, fiction and hypothesis which seems essential to its functioning as a scientific idiom. The function of this order of thinking in science is to facilitate the formulation of objective knowledge, knowledge of the laws of the relations between things. Here, all fiction is strictly subordinate to the rule of observation and verification. Comte now takes advantage of the fact that the sciences make use of imaginative inventions and fictions (as long as they are under powerful methodological controls). He does not make an absolute rule or definition as to the epistemological nature of fictions at this point, since he wants to suggest that once an order of scientific investigation is established only then is it possible for it to form the basis of a new order of practical elaborations. Instead of thinking that scientific progress was a linear process of moving from subjective empirical knowledge to an objective theoretical knowledge, it could now be suggested that the problem really relates to the way observation, classification and explanation occur and combine in any practice, indeed in any culture. Comte was thus led in the System, to suggest that there was first regime of knowledge (which he termed 'first and direct causality' (SPP, III, 133) involving a direct approach to objects ('as fetishes' (ibid.: 145)), out of which arose, through rationalisation the hidden divinities of polytheism and monotheism – entailing the dispersion of causes into an inaccessible and hidden realm (the regime of a 'second causality').

Here Comte's analysis comes as a surprise, since the formulations in this second period argue that the fetishistic conceptions of phenomena 'being direct and concrete, were profoundly real …' and as such they had a 'certain objectivity' so that 'the hypotheses employed were … verifiable' (ibid.). Indeed when the full development of the second, the subjective, causality was achieved in theisms, the only restraint on the influence of the arbitrary and hypothetical beings it produced as ruling wills was the more basic and fundamental fetishistic fatalism (SPP, III, 136). This fatalism clearly now seems to be re-conceptualised as an early and essential if primitive form of positivism and prop of all subsequent metaphysics. It is a theology concerned with Gods which develops the 'subjective' dimension in depth, and provides the basis for a genre of theorising 'which deals principally with *phenomena*'. The aim of theologism is to produce a 'foreknowledge of the presiding wills by carefully observing the various effects they produce.' He suggests that 'the plurality of the Gods was always indispensable for this theoretic objective.' The creation of these 'purely chimerical … preliminary beings' (p. 152) led to the deepening of the subjective life and to recourse to explanation through indirect causation: the human soul, will and self are introjections from the period dominated by such a social epistemology of indirect causation.

This discussion clarifies considerably the Comtean notion of the *phenomenon* as an object depending on the combined action of both the objective (at base fetishistic) and subjective methods where the action of imaginary hidden beings and powers becomes greatly amplified. And this can work in two ways, either through an explanation of the world by reference to hidden gods or one god, or by reference to hidden forces of nature, or hidden social forces conceived in a secular manner. It is through the complex interaction of objective and subjective methods that the opposition of practice and theory is established in the set of divisions which are installed in his concept of the metaphysical regime or the 'third causality' (SPP, III, 253). Here the hidden gods of theology are transformed into what he terms a metaphysical 'ontology' of entities and forces. In effect Comte theorises degrees of subjectivisation which arise up against the relative advances brought about by the sciences and the attempts to systematise them. He is however quite explicit in his estimation of the sequence of the emergence of these forms of subjectivity. This deepening is not progression. The only progression here lies with the rise of the sciences and their definition of what counts as reality.

Each science is established in a domain under the control of a methodology appropriate for its object. Previously he held that in cultures where the world of objects is continuous with living wills no separate science can be tolerated, he now suggests that it is only here the seeds of scientific reasoning can be found (Lévi-Strauss, 1972: 164, 220). Where the human world is governed by indirect wills of Gods or equivalent entities, again, the proto sciences of this world can exist only in a conflict since the dominant culture tries to prevent them developing. Science arises under conditions when its objects cease to be ruled by capricious hidden wills (which are attributions of human thoughts and affections projected as supernatural wills (SPP, III, 243)); and where there is only a search for law-governed relations not a search for absolute origins (the 'mode of production') of things or their ultimate and absolute causes. Social science makes headway when the objective method appropriate to its own domain becomes available, and when the ruling harmony and consensus of the theocratic state is broken. Sociology arises out of the conditions made possible by the earlier sciences, particularly astronomy and physics, in their struggles with theology.

If at the end of the Course in 1842, after twelve years of work, Comte had not really been happy with the conclusions of his sociological analysis and from the perspective adopted here, it is not difficult to see why. There was a lingering doubt that not all was well. Having built the vast edifice on the speculative challenge of the positive state, the sociology is still in essence a hypothesis awaiting its confirmation or disconfirmation. Having constructed a system of *jalons fondamentaux*, the fundamental signposts, it was still too early in 1842 to say in any detail exactly in which direction they were pointing. The sociology constructed in the Course took the risk of having a rhetorical structure of verifiable propositions. A decade later, at the end of the third volume of System, Comte wrote triumphally:

> the fundamental theory stands completed and confirmed. The laws originally deduced from an abstract examination of human nature have been demonstrated to be real laws, explaining the entire course of the destinies of the human species. Sociology has, for each epoch in turn, exhibited the present as the necessary outcome of the past, and so has enhanced its own authority by a continuous accumulation of decisive proofs.
>
> ([1853] SPP, III, 535)

But was there a continuous accumulation of proofs?

The key analyses presented in Comte's works are to be found in book five of the Course (1841), and volume three of the System (1853). They cover roughly the same ground, in the same order but with significant differences of emphasis and analysis. The reading of European history is normative, in the sense that the theory of the normal state is a starting point for the narrative and controls the construction of the final stage as that of fetishism and positivism. In between these two types are social forms dominated by the principal stage of intellectual evolution. It is one thing to construct a genealogy of the sciences showing that each branch of knowledge passes in a revolutionary break from theological to positive forms, and that each science is formed in a specific order; it is quite another to show that in general the whole of human history is cumulative in the same way, and is determined by the same progressive law. In fact the argument is that progression in one of the sequences is the motor that drives history in its entirety through a series of profound conflicts and convulsions. What is evident in the later writings is a much more systematic attempt to delineate the historical sequence of socio-cultural accumulation on the one hand, and the character of the formations in the non-progressive sequence.

What Comte presented in 1841 is, an abstract genealogy (his search for the *jalons fondamentaux*). His order of exposition:

A an introductory theory: the laws of social development
B social analyses in the following order:
  i fetishism
  ii polytheism – Egyptian, Greek, Roman
  iii monotheisms
  iv metaphysical state: decomposition series
  v metaphysical state: organic series
  vi the French Revolution
C a concluding survey.

What Comte presents however a decade later, in 1853 is a general account of the theory of normal states of society, followed by an attempt to periodise the whole of European history from fetishism to the positive polity in terms of regimes of causality:

A an introductory presentation of the laws of social development and the normal state;
B the social analyses in the following order:
  i fetishism
  ii theocracy (Egyptian polytheism)
  iii Greek polytheism
  iv Roman polytheism
  v Catholic Middle ages
  vi The Western Crisis – its twofold movement
C a summary of the process of cultural and social accumulation.
D a whole volume (vol. IV) is then devoted to outlining in detail:
  vii the Positive Polity: fetishism-positivism.

The main differences between the expositional forms are therefore, first the treatment of the stage of polytheism becomes greatly expanded, but second, that of the metaphysical state is contracted. The 1853 genealogies are also, third, more inclusive, for they now embrace intellectual, practical and affective series in preparation for the final religion of love to come. This analysis holds that whatever the specific contribution of any one *regime,* say the Roman contribution to social accumulation, it is always the intellectual order which takes precedence in the classification, even though Comte now begins to point out that the social order was based primarily on its military organisation, in the practical series, that is where the process of rationalisation was primarily at work.

Where previously Comte's aim was to harmonise the system of the different branches of knowledge and to produce an ethics from the last science in the chain (sociology), the function of the sociology in the new perspective is to predict the practical and affective elements and organisational forms which will make up the final stage of society itself. The new religious cult anticipates the new state.

In this perspective, therefore, what becomes significant is the way that different societies, functioning under different conditions, make quite unique contributions to the cumulative progress of Humanity. Societies are not equally creative, nor in the same ways. Some are important as cultural carriers (Comte notes that the Romans inherited the Greek sciences and carried them alongside their culture, as did the Arab societies afterwards, without these sciences becoming the dominant organising societal principle directly). Societies are complex admixtures of different principles, and with the exception of the metaphysical type, always established on the basis of a single fundamental principle but where the key process of rationalisation can occur in one or more of the three series (intellect, practice, affect). The passages between the various stages of theologism, though he sometimes refers to them as revolutions (especially between fetishism and polytheism) are not comparable in scale with the great revolution which starts in the West at the end of the Catholic period and marks the end of 'theology' itself as the effective organising principle. The structure of accumulation is not a linear one in any simple sense, since the revolution does not continue the theological and metaphysical trends into the final state: it is a revolution that displaces them because their formation throughout has been external and in opposition to them. In order to draw up a picture of the post-revolutionary society, one that has an organising principle with the same degree of effectiveness as that of theology, he presents a theory of creative, carrier, and of course destructive milieux as a framework for the theory of the positive tradition as a religious heritage.

In 1853 Comte drew attention to his thesis that there are in fact three great transitions: the first he identified as that of the Egyptian and Persian theocracy which degenerated into a closed and sterile culture; the second was that of Greece broke away from the first line to develop intellectually an 'evolution peculiar to the West' when it combined with the social achievements of Rome; the 'combined result' of this evolution was the third transition of the Catholic age (SPP, III, 534).

THE SHIFTS IN HIS POSITION BETWEEN THE COURSE AND THE SYSTEM

The social system

The first thing that strikes the reader in turning to the discussion of statics, is whereas previously Comte had discussed the social order in terms of the union (the family) and the association (and government) here the social organism is paradigmatically 'religion'. Religion (*religare*) is defined in terms of the unity of humankind. The definition derives not from a distinction between the sacred and the profane, but between the unity that includes both the union of the family and the greater unity of the society more generally. Curiously this is followed by a discussion which introduces a 'thought experiment' – what would social evolution look like if human beings had no material wants? His answer to this interesting question is that very probably, driven purely by feeling and intellectual rationalisation, human progression would pass from the third to the final state without passing through the metaphysical state at all (SPP, II, 122ff.). Something of a reinterpretation of the effectiveness of theology and metaphysical philosophy is indicated in these pages, which strongly suggest that in the metaphysical period itself, society finds its unity not from a moral but from a material order. Indeed the discussions of the Middle Ages again quickly arrive at new conclusions that the Christian doctrines were not sufficiently coherent to hold society together at the social level because they were based on a purely egoistic morality – it was the feudal order itself combined with Christianity which brought about the main advances in Europe. These are striking observations considering the whole problematic of the later Comte is expressly announced as having moved into the religious idiom – only as it seems to make it clear that 'religion' in this terminology has no simple relation to 'theology'.

The family is dealt with in a far more analytic manner. Whereas before it was a question of 'union' in 1852 it is examined from the point of view of its main relationships centring around the conjugal relation. The other relations are examined in terms of fraternity, etc., and the division between emotion and intellect. But the key change is that now women are no longer reduced to eternal childhood, but become the principal moral authority in the domestic sphere (read either as a goddess (Ritzer), as the 'nun in the family' (Dijksta) or as equivalent to the 'illustrious dead' (Vernon)). Instead, then, of passing to forms of association, Comte next introduces discussions of language and property as the 'tissues' of the social organism that tie the individual to culture on the one hand and to the earth on the other. In the metaphysical period there are apparent anomalies: the material order prevails, but more significantly at the political level the nation state mushrooms out of control because of the absence of a regulating authority. The true social organism is centred not on the nation, but on the city, under the spiritual authority of a universal priesthood – the church itself. The temporal process of government (after Hobbes, SPP, II, 242–50) possesses powers located in the city based on material force and relationships organised on duties not rights (citizenship is replaced with a regime of civil servants), but the spiritual power rests on moral authority and it is supreme in the subjective life (Acton, 1974).

What Comte opens up here is a whole new dimension of social control acting not on the objectively real, but on the subjective empire of the living dead. Vernon, however, raises the key point here which is to ask what could be Comte's model for these alterations to his statics? Careful textual reading shows that in the early writings and in the CPP Comte expressed no suggestion that the nation state itself was anomalous. In the SPP, however, well before Proudhon's better known version, 'the state literally vanishes even as a possible category' (1984: 553).The model for these ideas Vernon suggests convincingly is the 'City of God' of St Augustine 'fantastically reconstructed' (Vernon, 1984: 565). However there is something new in Comte's utopia according to this perceptive reading: 'Comte predicts in a sombre passage, the temporal leaders (*patriciat*) "secretly hate" the *sacerdoce* (priesthood) … a bitter though unavowable rivalry. The spiritual power is not only the object of the secret hatred of the patriciat, but is also unable to win more than the "cold respect" of its adversary, the proletariat' (Vernon, 1984: 559).

THE DYNAMICS

Fetishism

Comte's concept of fetishism as the first and basic starting point of the sociological series rests on the assumption that at this stage all the human faculties are in place and that in the course of social development no new faculties are added. Any special cultural developments among different peoples are not assumed (at this point) to rest on racial differences (1974b: 545–6). Instead of finding in fetishism a primary form of alienation, Comte establishes fetishism as creative of language, culture, social structure, and a social economy in which the first forms of domestication of animals, cultivation of plants, take place. Between 1840–2 and 1853 however a significant shift in Comte's assessment took place. In the earlier account he says 'it is in this form, above all others, that the religious spirit is most directly opposed to the scientific' (1974b: 551), while in the later one he says, in effect recognising the fundamental change of position: 'of the different forms of the fictitious synthesis, fetishism is logically and scientifically the best'. Indeed, between fetishism and positivism he discovers a radical identity. The first is spontaneous positivism, while the second is systematic. So Comte's view in 1853 suggests that 'it was only the intermediate regime instituted by theologism that was truly contrary to the general laws of human reason, although it was profoundly justified by social necessities' (SPP, III, 75). This is not a simple development of the thesis of the first account but a seismic shift in Comte's thought and assessment of the relations between the stages of development that is evident here, for now a new set of states is in place: first fetishistic, second theo-metaphysical (or theologism), and third positive, indicating a very radical reversal of earlier normative evaluations. He notes specifically that the 'high quality of fetishist philosophy is not seen by modern thinkers simply because they do not place themselves at the proper point of view' (ibid.: 77), for they value speculation (for example, the current metaphysics of the 'pompous verbiage of the proud German doctors' (p. 83)) over observation. The new demarcation in place is intended to show that the important social development of the speculative order during the theological stage led to the formation of the priesthood and its 'political authority' but not to a real increase in its speculative force (p. 83). Comte expresses this reversal directly: 'fetishism is theoretically superior to theologism in doctrine as well as in method, even as regards the inorganic world' (p. 74).

We can note the continued appeal to the controlling role of phrenology in establishing the 'normal' state. In 1841, the normal state had been established in a priori fashion from Gall's phrenology (1974b: 545), but by 1853 the architecture of this controlling theory had been completely revised following his moral and emotional 'regeneration'. It is evident in fact that this new point of view radicalises the whole of his theory of the three states in relation to its subdivisions and cumulative forms. There is no continuous progression but a series of conjunctural displacements and partial developments with an attempt to include alongside intellectual and practical genealogies, a tertiary genealogy of the emotions throughout the entire range of the sociological series. Essentially he rewrites the evaluation of fetishism as a survey of conditions in which emotion takes precedence over reason. He concludes that fetishism provides all societies with a permanent infrastructure of observational practice and emotional balance, common to all periods.[1]

Polytheism

Here Comte again drastically revises his analyses between the two studies. The initial sketch of the three kinds of polytheism is greatly extended. The Egyptian case is examined as a fundamentally conservative form which arises from a tradition of astrolatry out of which evolved the first priestly castes. It forms a theocratic state which achieves a systematisation of written language. It closes itself however into an oppressive regime from which the Greek regime (progressive and military) detaches itself. The Greek contribution to the cumulation process is strictly limited in this analysis to its intellectual creativity. Comte argues that this arose and was circumscribed by very precise conditions, indeed so restrictive of its development where these social constraints that the sciences were halted at a certain point 'for fifteen centuries' (SPP, III, 275). In effect he draws up a picture of the first impulses of positive knowledge and its clash with theology in a way which reveals an inevitable appearance of early metaphysics. His analysis now highlights the specific contribution of Aristotle who established the first forms of biology and sociology (SPP, III, 253). The obstacles to further development came from theological closure as the new theory of the motion of the earth struck at its fundamental doctrines and social power (p. 176). Roman society specifically develops the activity dimension of the series while it carries, without developing, the intellectual achievements of the Greeks (p. 299).

In 1840–2, Comte had noted that in analysing Greek and Roman societies he intended to promote them into the abstract space of the theoretical series as key examples of variations on the way the concrete analysis could be made. In fact he spent little time on the Roman example. In 1853, however the discussion is greatly extended. In the first place however he makes another important theoretical comment: why classify the Roman case as polytheistic, if its fundamental development is social and not intellectual? His answer, worth citing, is that it is because:

> all the mental functions are radically identical in the speculative and the practical order of the mind; which differ only in the relative intensity of meditation as compared with contemplation, or of deduction as opposed to induction. Their outward contrast is mainly due to a diversity of habits determined by a difference of aim.
>
> (SPP, III, 297)

He then remarks that his reassessment of the Roman case is parallel to that of his rethinking on fetishism:

> The fundamental similarity between the theoretic and the practical reason is never so clearly shown as in relation to a mode of activity

> which incessantly calls for the most vigorous concentration of inductive and deductive operations of every kind. (p. 297)

The Roman situation was one in which concrete reason could be and was applied above all to social ends.

His re-evaluations continue. His new estimate of the Roman and Catholic periods is dramatically evident when he writes:

> The social sympathies were actively stimulated by the eminently civic character of Roman life … as if the normal preponderance of the affections had been explicitly recognised. When the new stimulus of Catholicism came proclaiming at last after its fashion this supreme rule, its influence on practical life tended to lead us away from our real *human* unity, which was more nearly approached by the Roman synthesis.
>
> (SPP, III, 298)

What Comte tries to achieve here and in the analysis to follow is to show how his category of the polytheistic regime functions as an explanatory basis for the Roman development of the 'normal' social order, indeed now estimated to be more important than monotheistic regimes. The way he does this is to emphasise the primacy of the military purposes in the Roman case which exercised its discipline over the other activities, the exigencies of the aims of the temporal power and practical life curbing 'speculative vagaries' (SPP, III, 300). Roman polytheism becomes more systematic, as an effect of the increasing rationality of its political and military organisation, not its intellectual organisation.

Monotheism

As a result of his changed assessment of fetishism and Roman polytheism, Comte also has changes to make to his assessment of the Catholicism of the middle ages. In the account of 1840–2 he emphasised the separation of powers between the spiritual and temporal orders established by Catholicism and outlined a thesis that the moral regeneration of the west was led by the papacy. It also posed the question that although the triumph of Catholicism took ten centuries to come into existence; it lasted only between Gregory VII and Boniface VIII, two centuries at its height. It witnessed the practical transition from slavery, through serfdom to emancipation. It also witnessed the great flowering of the epoch of chivalry.

But when Comte turned to this period again in 1853, he was at pains to explain why he was still using the category of monotheism to classify medieval Europe, for he had concluded by now that it was important 'to show distinctly the radical incapacity of theological doctrine for any true coordination of human affairs' (SPP, III, 354). He reports that further consideration confirms that comparing the different forms of monotheism (Judaic, Christian and Islamic) the division of powers in the West now on close analysis appears to be the result of Catholicism's conjunctural situation, not its monotheistic doctrine. It is also the case that if monotheism seemed to restore the heart to its proper leading position this too was not intrinsic, but a 'result of external influences' (SPP, III, 355). A sociological analysis of the Catholic organisation in the Middle Ages shows that its function was to develop new modes of strictly moral regulation over the elements which were already in existence. Whereas earlier theological forms had developed a spontaneous priestly caste, medieval Catholicism developed an attempt to control social life through consent based on a priestly corporation now regulated systematically. As the monotheistic doctrine was incapable of an effective and consistent discipline, social regulation was achieved through the benevolence and wisdom of the priesthood. In effect Comte here only draws out elements which were already implied in his earlier analysis of the divergent structures of other monotheisms, but previously Catholic doctrine had been seen as responsible for having brought about the key development of the separation of spiritual and temporal powers.

Comte ends his discussion of the monotheistic phase with a long analysis of the history of Western feudalism from the fourth century. The analysis is certainly not concerned with the 'second causality' or with monotheistic doctrines. Its main interest is now a more focused analysis of the formation of the social function of the catholic priesthood in consensual moral government of feudal society. This change of emphasis turns the whole of Comte's analysis of the monotheistic phase into a vast paradox. In having attempted to show the speculative evolution from polytheism to monotheism creates an inaccessible realm of causality that forms a focus for social organisation, he discovers that all the effective historical elements and processes in the sociological genealogy lie elsewhere: in science, in feudal development, in the governmental practices of a priesthood; not in the functioning of monotheistic theology which now appears merely to be a superstructure.

Deism

A significant further reconstruction occurs with the analysis of the metaphysical state. We know that the positive state lies in the future. It is none the less accorded the full utopian treatment of a whole volume, the fourth, of the System. We know that the metaphysical state which is a state which has existed since the fourteenth century, has also been described as having no coherent principle of its own, is purely transitional, and hybrid. But having sketched the double movement which characterises it in the opuscules, Comte did not abandon his early conception altogether. He reworked it. In the 1820s he had set out two separate historical series, the first called 'The Decline of the Old Social System' (1974a: 82–90) and the second 'The Growth of the New Social System' (pp. 91–108). The scope of the history is from the eleventh century when the old system was in full vigour. There then followed a period when the new system was preparing itself and it made its appearance in the sixteenth century with an attack on the spiritual powers, in the seventeenth on the temporal powers, and a final and 'decisive' attack in the eighteenth 'determining the fall of the theologico-military system' (1974a: 90).

THE NEW ACCOUNT OF THE LAW OF THE THREE STATES

In 1853 Comte changed the form of exposition for the theory of this transition, the so-called twofold movement. In place of separate discussions of the fall of the old regime and then the rise of the new, Comte presented the four phases one after the other in blocks and the discussion sub-divides each phase into its declining and positive aspects. In effect it seems clear that he had very great difficulty in thinking through the sociological analysis of Western societies except in a schizoid form, a Manichaen struggle. This fragmented form of exposition breaks up the long view of the transition and the general concept of the metaphysical state disappears from the presentation, though it is clear from the subheadings, the content of the phases are almost exactly the same. Indeed even the separation of the French Revolutionary epoch from the other periods is maintained, and Comte very noticeably retains the two systems of dating, the first more general, 1300, 1500, the other, from 1789, concrete historical events.

Is this whole period the metaphysical stage, and how does the law of the three states now explain it? The conceptualisation of this state is remarkably consistent in its content. The function of the metaphysical philosophy is to act as a purely negative but general critique of theology. But in 1853 Comte introduces a change in the relation between monotheistic thought and metaphysics:

> The corrosive action peculiar to metaphysics comes out when it tries to dominate theologism instead of modifying it by a gradual dissolution. But so long as ontology remains subordinated to

> theology its purely negative character is kept in check, and it gives rise only to useful transformations which do not destroy all efficiency for organisation. Such was the case in the middle ages. At bottom polytheism is the only true theological state, because there alone imagination reigned without control. Monotheism is always the result of an essentially metaphysical theology which pares down fiction by rationalising.
>
> (SPP, III, 54–5)

In fact, as I have already shown above in the discussion of polytheism, theology is limited not just by metaphysics but also by the structures of fetishistic fatalism. What Comte works towards then is a theory of the combination of states, and that revolutions are reversals of an order of dominance, and that the edifice of monotheism in the West as a single effective theological whole is an illusion.

What concerns us here is the specific analysis of this exceptional state of transition, for what he introduces is essentially an attempt at reading European history from a sociological point of view located now within a religious framework. The final state is now no longer considered as secular but the triumph of religion over science in a polity. There remains a very precise difficulty: previously Comte held that there was a radical discontinuity between the metaphysical and the positive state: the crucial rupture in the modern transition is between the rising series (industry and science, positivism), and the decomposition series: from Protestantism through to Deism. The whole rationale for Comte's enormous methodological inventions was that in applying them the true lineage could be identified: the rising sequence would not lead from theologism, through Deism to Humanism or Pantheism. The future would arise out of the positive series in a polity where science would play the leading role.

This reading reveals why it is so important in Comte's view that European history is regarded as a combination of two irreconcilable systems, one declining and one rising. It reveals the essential role of the argument that the metaphysical elements and structures belong to the old order, as modifications induced in it by the underlying forces of the new forces which are yet to complete their formation into a social organism. The argument hangs on the thesis that there is no crucial rupture between theology and metaphysics. Metaphysical phenomena are, according to Comte's analysis, completely dependent on the prior organisations of the feudo-Catholic order, and also, fundamentally for their legitimation, on the true agency, the positive order in *statu nascendi*. Metaphysical phenomena are transdetermined in principle: they are symptoms of the formation of new forces in the system and they do not form a social organism or the basis for a social organism on their own. Indeed Comte now conceives of a monotheism-metaphysics coupling. Since the facts as they are experienced within any situation are complex and interwoven, a rational reconstruction is essential for any adequate understanding at the scientific level to become possible: the construction of such series must proceed to make them as pure and homogeneous and as extensive as possible. If the key to reading Comtean sociology lies in understanding the way that the theory, the law of the three states, enables the sociologist to periodise an abstract history, to establish the signposts, the *jalons fondamentaux,* the shift to religion and the introduction of the Religion of Humanity creates a theoretical problem. Can this new 'Supreme Being', and Comte refers to Humanity in the feminine, be thought other than in relation to the metaphysical genealogy, other Supreme Beings? In what way is the metaphysical Deity fundamentally different from the positive Deity? The logic of Comte's position seems to point to the development of the three state law: the phenomena of the post-Deist episodes of the metaphysical period deprived of their hidden essences become the basis of what might be called a fetishism (Comte retains a Trinity of fetishes) through which positivism (post-humanism) achieves its hegemony.

10

Sociologists and the Regime of Fetishes

The logic of Comte's second career becomes clear in the 1848 Discourse. Unlike the Discourse of 1844 (which was a preface to a treatise on geometry) it is essentially an introduction to sociology in a religious mode. But in order to read and locate the motor in Comte's theory it is essential to bear in mind that all the description of the positive polity itself lies in the realm of fiction, the ideal type; it is utopian writing, and expressly so. But he attempts to complete the prediction of his theory by his own actions in inaugurating the final cult, opening what has classically has called 'the paradox of prediction' (Friedrichs, 1972: 177–89). Once Comtean theory fell into this paradox, his sociology would inevitably become sterile.

To find a way out of this paradox and to examine Comte's theoretical sociology in a new way, it has been necessary to put to one side all the 'reality effects' called into existence by the attempt to ground the theoretical 'series' in a closed narrative history. And this can be done against the theoretical backdrop of his theory of utopias as a theoretical instrument (as well as a religious promise). As Michel Houellebecq, who continues novelists' interest in Comte from George Eliot, H.G. Wells and others, recently remarked 'everything in the political and moral thought of Comte seems to have been made in order to exasperate the contemporary reader … we have not today left the metaphysical epoch, and less than ever have any intention of leaving it'; that today it might appear that far from being a period of transition characterised by the dissolution of theologies it has become a period in which theologies 'are maintained artificially by means of the uncertainty inherent in all metaphysics' (in Bourdeau *et al.*, 2003: 7).

But if understanding the theory of the metaphysical state is indeed the key to unlocking Comte's sociology there are still theoretical problems to be solved. One way of examining these problems is to look at the work of Michel Serres. The curious aspect of Serres' work on Comte is that from his introductory essay of 1975 to Comte's *Course in Positive Philosophy* through to his later writings (most notably his 1995 essay 'Paris 1800'), Serres passes through the same trajectory as Comte himself – that is to say from an objective to a subjective and religious method. Serres became more and more sympathetic to that part of Comte's work which has been most reviled. The earlier essay of 1975 suggests that Comte's account of the sciences is based on a mode of explanation which is derived from a primitive mechanical model of movement, conceived in terms of forces acting on a point such that it describes a linear motion. Serres calls this the 'motor' which Comte uses to analyse the circles of revolutionary movement he finds everywhere. Serres wrongly locates the direct source of Comte's model in Louis Poinsot's book *Eléments de Statique* of 1837, (in fact it was in place in Comte's writings from a different source at a much earlier phase). Here the idea of statics is that of a stable point where two opposed forces are in equilibrium. Rotation, that is revolution, is induced where the forces are unequal and applied so that the wheel turns. For Serres this explains why Comte thinks in terms of the couple theology-science, for the motor is precisely these two opposed forces which in their action describe the orbits of the law of the three states, for in each of Comte's analysis the same thing is always found, the revolutionary circle of the action Serres identifies as the action of the two forces, progress and order. This means that Comte does not have, for Serres, a radical theory of state-transformation. Comte's is a theory of vectors, in which there can be only circles, and then spirals which form transitions between one circle and another (in Comte, 1975: I, 18). What may happen of course is that there is a moment of stasis, and the progression of circular movement may become blocked when the two forces are applied directly on the same point, equal and opposite, stopping history at a moment of permanent crisis (p. 18); reproducing the familiar critique by Karl Popper, Serres says all movement in Comte's account revolves around fixed central points. This conservative static model was decisively replaced in the industrial period, when Carnot's theory of heat produced a different idea of revolution, revolutionary state-transformations.

Serres' later writings, when he places Comte's work in the context of the scientific revolution in France around 1800, suggest a modification of this reading. His argument is that this revolution effectively replaced the religious clergy, with a new scientific elite: 'with the French Revolution, the scientists come to power' (Serres, 1995b: 422). He sketches a list of the main authors of this revolution in mathematics, astronomy, physics and chemistry, Biology and medicine (pp. 425–7). The new elite, he says, was led by 'a geometer who rose to the heights of military and political power. His name was Bonaparte, and he had solved what was called Napoleon's problem: to divide a circle into four equal parts by means of compasses alone … The Emperor embodied … the victorious struggles of the sciences against the humiliated humanities'. Serres concludes that 'during the Revolution, this totality (of scientists) constituted the equivalent of a Council of Ministers' (1995b: 428–9). This was the period of great treatises, typical of which were those by Lagrange on Mechanics, and on Analytical Functions. Each of these begin with an encyclopaedic summation of previous knowledge, what Serres calls a 'double integration': that is they are at the same time historical and dogmatic, science and history from this period go together. The characteristic view of this epoch is that, the world is a system (Laplace), governed by universal gravitation (Newton), and the movement of the elements in this world is cyclical and 'engraved in differential equations' so the world is at base a stable one which 'turns and returns to itself, indefinitely' (p. 435). But there are two elements here, two revolutions: the first are the '-ologies' -those disciplines in which the revolution returns to the same point, the second are the '-ogonies' which describe irreversible processes of development (biology and geology should be biogony and geogony, and perhaps we could add sociogony). And there are those disciplines which combine in more complex ways the two together. Thus with Lamarck's concept of evolution: life's plan is complicated by external causes and these make it irreversible. But it turns out that 'the men of the Revolution were conservative scientists' since in all the fields surveyed from mathematics to biology, all were static in basic formation in 1800. Modern science does not date from this period in any of these disciplines.

Thus he says Comte's work should be read as belonging to a very specific configuration. It reflects and belongs to it; it puts its major elements together in order to complete it as a system. Serres concludes:

> I believe that … he is codifying an idea or a feeling which one can read or experience in the works and lives, in the social and

> speculative activities of the scientists who lived through the French Revolution, who were at Paris in the year 1800. Their great treatises, in general, first of all recapitulate the internal history of their respective disciplines, then lay it out according to a systematic plan: progress, then order. Fourier, Laplace, Lavoisier, Haüy, Lamarck, Monge and twenty others knew or felt that they were entering into a new time in which rational science would become the crucial social factor, which would dominate education, the army, industry and agriculture, which in their turn would produce the preconditions of reason: scientific order determines social progress whose order determines scientific progress. Their universal science led them to a unique sociopolitical location through an acute moment of crisis which would give rise at the same time to history, science and society. Comte sanctifies this unique double experience, occupying all the positions at the same time.
>
> (1995b: 452–3)

What increasingly appeals to Serres is Comte's universalism expressed through his encyclopaedic Religion of Humanity: 'people laugh at the late Comte without having read any … (for) positivism turns out to be weak where it is believed to be strong, precisely with regard to science and history, and strong in the areas where everyone condemns it, like an understanding of religion' (p. 448). Take for example the famous positivist calendar, he says, it is 'tolerant, pluralist and secular … a spell for inter-cultural reconciliation. That's why it didn't succeed' (p. 449). If we examine the new religion in more detail it seems clear that Serres is wrong, and that far from being a pluralistic religion, the fetishistic Religion of Humanity radically excludes the practice of polytheism, monotheism and all forms of metaphysical religion because they are all absolute religions. The cult of the new religion acknowledges their role in human evolution, as steps along the route, but not in themselves as having made any progressive contribution. In fact, given Comte's new definition, they are not religious at all.

THE NEW GRAND NARRATIVE IN THE SUBJECTIVE MODE

As I have shown Comte radically overhauled his conception of the Western transition in respect to gender, emotions, and in relation to religion itself. Comte seemed to become painfully aware that the sequence, theology–metaphysics–positivity, had to be looked at again in a radically new way. The problems were multiple. First, the emergence of the division between the spiritual and the temporal (fundamental to his perspectives from the start) in the Christian Middle Ages was not inherent in the law itself, since other monotheisms did not exhibit the logic this separation. Second, having performed the operation of making the final science appear at its appointed time, sociology itself seemed incapable of provoking the instant rallying point for a new politics and a new political order he anticipated: reason, intellect, was not enough. Third, the scientific community showed no sign of coming together to form some vast association of its own accord; in fact the sciences were undergoing rapid and revolutionary change sweeping away the science matrix of 1800 (Serres) and dispersing them into even more divergent specialisms. This meant, fourth, that there was a problem in the way that the genealogical lines, his 'series', were to be reconceived, since the positive sequence of industry and the sciences did not seem to be leading directly to any unique morality or polity of its own. The utopia Comte now elaborated was a patchwork of medieval and modern elements, designed to produce a maximal contrast with the current political scene. Much of the writing in the 1848 Discourse is an attempt at producing a programmed transition through the metaphysical period. But the analysis is haunted by the question: were the basic series of his analysis of modern history misconceived right from the very start? What precisely would be the relation between metaphysical humanism and the principle of the sovereignty of the people as its legitimating political principle on the one hand, and the Religion of Humanity on the other? In this perspective the struggle of methodologies becomes a war between Gods or rather between two humanisms: metaphysical humanity and post-metaphysical Humanity.

There seems to be crucial elements in the final period which play the role of maintaining his basic propositions. These elements are the key definitions of terms in his emerging theory: religion, love, humanity, the positive polity, freedom, fetishism, altruism. In place of the idea that society becomes less religious as it moves into the positive epoch, Comte suggests that it becomes even more religious – religion is redefined as '*religare*' rebinding, rather than as a system of worship and ethics orientated towards a transcendental sacred order. All social systems that have a single coherent moral order legitimated by an ethical discipline can be called religious in this sense. It is thus no accident that following in this tradition, Durkheim could use the phrase 'religion of humanity'[1] out of which others could generalise a theory of secular 'civic religion'. But for Comte, becoming more religious would mean becoming more morally organised.

New and crucial definitions now also come in relation to love, and love of Humanity. Because Comte argued that the main enemy of the positive polity was theology and metaphysics, the last place we would expect him to look for a concept of love was the Christian tradition, particularly love of Jesus. Yet he did find it there in the works of the mystics, particularly Thomas à Kempis, because read carefully it seems clear that this text advocates a complete renunciation of the self: 'a man has to renounce everything and then to renounce himself… to have no vestige left of love for self' (1977: 89). He said brusquely, all you have to do in reading these works is to substitute the concept 'Humanity' for God 'without ever forgetting his provisional services' (1891a: 294). Humanity is not like a conventional deity since it is something that can be shown to exist, it is not a non-empirical reality. Comte's epistemology had however to go further, since it is also possible to show that Nature exists and he was opposed on epistemological grounds to pantheistic nature worship. His solution was to argue for a particular kind of nature worship, one that radically eliminated any notion of a hinter world of hidden deities. This was to return to the earliest religious mode: a fetishistic adoration of certain objects of nature.

His later religious ideas thus make some major steps away from some of his earlier pronouncements. His criticisms of the fetishism of the Saint-Simonians, of the 'vagaries' of philosophers like Newton, of vitalism, all now fade, while his criticisms of 'theology' where there is worship of hidden gods, and metaphysics, where there are hidden forces, are, paradoxically, strengthened. The new religion is not 'fusional' – it is a carefully composed combination of elements and methods. Fetishism and positivism unite in eliminating hidden essences, forces, spirits, and all hidden deities. In the new religion these are simply transformed into apparent, visible, sensual, immediate objects. Love does not require sentiment, or understanding, but knowledge, attachment and devotion. His extreme, altruistic, love requires complete elimination of the metaphysical egoistic self. The implication politically is the withdrawal of all structures that prop up the inordinate egoism of modern society, particularly the doctrine of possessive individualism and human rights. Comte goes to the other extreme, the almost total elimination of 'human rights'. His alternative is the promotion of 'human duties'. Crimes against Humanity are crimes resulting in the dereliction of duties, a failure of altruism. The later works become subjective in the sense that they are socio-centric, or Humano-centric. Not only are they written from the perspective of Humanity, they are also lived subjectively within Humanity in time and space. Following with precision his definition of truth as that which if all conditions are conducive, can be demonstrated he concludes that this is not yet a demonstrated religion; it is in principle however a demonstrable religion. 'Humanity' has yet to find its own identity.

It is important to remember here that Comte's argument is that what he is describing is the true outcome of the logic of the contestation between science and theology. In effect it is an account of the situation that will be brought about by the action of the progression of positivity. Comte is simply extrapolating the consequences of the rise of science in completing the process of eliminating metaphysics, admitting now that the possibility of making every element of life positive would not only be an impossibility, attempting it would lead to a situation in conflict with the basic makeup of Humanity itself. Read in this way, his analysis is suggestive: his account is a variation on the way that scientific knowledge and technology alter culture in the modern crisis. This constitutes something of setback for Comte's overall ambitions. Not only can he not find in the sciences any principle of unity except at the level of methodology, he cannot find any principle of the unity of a future culture except from within pagan fetishism. The logic of his argument is that in the end the effective rise of positivity drives out all theology and metaphysics except the fetish. But the end is a far way off, since it is evident that the procession of the law has stopped at the metaphysical stage, with a stand-off between the new positivity-fetishism couple on the one side against the theology-metaphysics 'couple' on the other.

Is this the new formulation of the law of the three states reached at the end of Comte's work? If so, the trajectory of the law would be the following: from a law that was essentially an account of the European transition from feudalism to industrialism; through a law of three stages, feudalism, legalism-deism, positivism; to a law of two series, monotheism to metaphysics, positivity to positive polity; and finally, to a law of two series – of monotheism to metaphysics, fetishism to positivity-fetishism. The particular sequence of the religious series would change:

First formulations:	I (fetishism, polytheism, and monotheism), II (metaphysics), III positivism;
Transitional sequence:	I (fetishism), II ('onto-theologism' that includes metaphysics), III (positivism);
Final sequence:	I (fetishism), II ('theologism'), III (positivity-fetishism).

Clearly at this stage, Comte required a completely reconstructed theory of fetishism.

A RETURN TO THE 'KINGDOM OF DARKNESS' (HOBBES (1946: 397–459))?

As Comte's thinking in the realm of neo-fetishism developed he began to experiment in ways which were immediately criticised (by Mill and Littré) as legitimising a return to superstition. Today the same kind of debate is in progress, probably led by Baudrillard's explicit return to the use of fetishism and the use of terms like fatal theory, seduction, destiny, evil, (his brilliant doctoral 'habilitation' was an exercise in this mode (Baudrillard, 1988)). Baudrillard has drawn attention to the new superficiality of modern culture, something that Horkheimer had noticed about Comte's epistemology (Horkheimer, 1972: 37). The messianic frame is variously adopted in the work of Virilio, and Derrida. This mode is also explored by Serres and Latour (especially Latour's notion of the 'factish' (1999)) and in the recently efforts of neo-vitalists. It haunts, if I may use the term, all the discussions around the issue of the inhuman, and the post-human. It is an issue prominent in the work of Maffesoli (1993), who has also supervised and controversially overseen the doctoral work of astrologist Elisabeth Tessier, famous throughout France for her horoscopes (her doctoral thesis read the horoscopes of the sociological theorists (for an account of her work and the challenge to the validity of her doctorate, see Lahire, 2005: 351– 87; the title of his essay is 'Une astrologue sur la planet des sociologies, ou comment devenir docteur en sociologie sans posséder le métier de sociologue?)). Obviously there is a parallel between the questions of 'historical inevitability', prediction, foresight-anticipation (Friedrichs, 1972: 177ff.) and that of prophecy, the promise, the work of 'seers' (Friedrichs, p. 65 – see his 'death of prophecy', p. 71). In the current debate over the inhuman in France, the question could be examined from the point of view of the nature of the object – is it alive? Does it have sovereignty over us? Can it be domesticated or not? Comte's answer appears to develop the practice of the neutralisation and domestication under the control of a new priesthood.

Although he began to dabble in certain mild forms of re-enchanting culture, for example writing his final volume through an acrostic grid (see Kremer-Marietti, 1982: 234–51; cf. Baudrillard, 1993: 195–213), it was clear that certain fetishistic forms were nevertheless to be prohibited in the new order. The most evident in the last volume of SPP, the earliest, in many ways, the most curious of these prohibitions was against what was defined as 'fatalism'. But in his last work the *Subjective Synthesis* (1856) a new relation between fetishism and fatalism was worked out. This work is written expressly for a new priesthood (1891b: vi) and cannot be appreciated, he pronounced, unless the perspective of its devotion to Humanity is acknowledged. It is, he says, 'composed under the supposition that I am writing in the year 1929, in my eyes the seventy-third year of the normal state' ((p. vii) – the year 1856 would be the commencement of the positive era).

This work was to be thought of as being written in 'a posthumous language'; he was 'occupying his tomb in anticipation' (1891b: viii). Our life, he says, now is one in which 'we ought habitually to live more with our ancestors and our descendents than with our contemporaries, requires that religion should bear on it throughout the stamp of subjectivity' (p. 44). The new combination of fetishism and positivism is possible on three conditions. The first is that positivism retains its predominance in the abstract spheres of thought, while fetishism remains active at the concrete. Second, the abstract level is that of invariable law, the concrete is recognised only as that of will. Curiously, third, the method of subordinating the fetishes is that concrete 'external bodies' are endowed 'with the faculties of feeling and acting, provided that we refuse them thought, so that their wills may always be blind' (1891b: 7). The idea of matter as inert, a 'theological prejudice' is overcome – and indeed also is the metaphysical prejudice towards 'fluids' 'which masked the true life of bodies' (1891b: 7), as long as these have no intellect. They are neutered and rendered comatose in order to take their place in the Religion of Humanity.

The world of objects is alive in an animistic, fetish culture. It takes a long time for cultures to divide the world into the animate and the inanimate – quite a different division between the world completely under the imaginary control of the subject and that which resists the subject (the so-called reality principle). For Comte the move to complete neo-fetishism involves the following: we may, he says, use our imagination to:

> suppose that the nature of the world was at one time more akin to that of man than it is now … it is allowable to suppose that our planet and the other habitable stars were endowed with intelligence before there was possible in them the development of society. At that time the earth devoted its strength to preparing the abode of Humanity, whose evolution could only take place on a planet dead from the exhaustion consequent on those efforts, proportionate rather to its material power than to its spiritual capacity … The earth during its period of intelligence was able to develop its physical and chemical activity so as to improve the astronomical order by a change in its principal coefficients. Our planet was able thus to make its orbit less eccentric, and consequently make itself

> more habitable by planning a long series of explosions analogous to those which produce comets.
>
> (1891b: 8–9)

This illustrates the possible future connection between fiction, poetry and demonstration.

THE POSITIVISTS INFORM THE POETS OF THEIR ROLE AND MISSION

Comte moved on to a second step, the 'final synthesis'. Fetishism having been neutered, is permitted as such to pass from the concrete to the abstract level (p. 12). The abstract theory of science then determines the overarching nature of the inevitable futures of all beings. Thus in the end Comte admits that a 'general destiny governs special fatalities' (1891b: 11–12) and fate makes its reappearance. The earth becomes the 'Great Fetish', the abode[2] of the 'Great Being' (Humanity):

> In the theological order, prayer is too self-regarding to invoke an inflexible order. Shut out from adoration, fate, despite its acknowledged sway, could not awake in the ancients regret for an omission in their religious system … fetishism was less unjust and more complete, especially when astrology attributed the general laws of the influences of the heavens. Positivism alone is able to honour the unchangeableness of the universal order … Humanity … should dispose us to revere the fate on which rests the whole of our existence.
>
> Under early fetishism the empire of fate could be adored only by assigning it to the stars. … Theologism weakened this worship by representing matter as passive, and masked moral order by the caprices of the gods. … Without the uninterrupted rule of destiny feeling would become vague, intellect unstable, and activity barren. […] When aided by the supreme fate, universal love can secure as a habitual result that personality submit to sociability.
>
> (1891b: 12–13)

The problem of modernity is the problem of resentment and rebellion. Comte proposes a theory of acceptance and submission, indeed one must learn to cherish submission (p. 14). The first dignified obedience was established in the Middle Ages (if it appeared to be to God, it was in fact to Humanity). The model of true voluntary submission however is to be found within the scientific tradition where it arises as a continuation of the primitive veneration of an inflexible destiny. Love is transcendental and 'should extend beyond the regulations we impose on ourselves'. And 'So viewed the leading characteristic of positive worship is the glorification of destiny … in the name of its moral efficacy' (1891b: 14–15). The objects of positive worship appear here as a new Trinity: Humanity, the World (not universe) and Destiny, or in the terms of the cult itself the Great Being, (Humanity), the Fetish (the earth), the Milieu (space). Originally worship rested on fear but now love is the cement of social solidarity. The problem of worshiping the World is only completed by recourse to the poetic. The profane sciences construct fictions such as inertia; the sacred sciences can now imagine the World in a sympathetic 'general medium'. The culture with the most developed idea of this medium was China (1891b: 19). It was powerful enough to prevent the development of theologism and a caste system. In China though, 'space is undistinguished from the sum of the heavenly bodies under the influence of astrology' (1891b: 19). A direct transition to positivity in China can be achieved merely by making this medium relative.

The final and perhaps ultimate idea in the new religion is a positive theory of the soul. Here the subjective method is given reign within the constraints established by the objective (phrenological) theory of the brain. There are no hidden essences here, the results of intellect and emotion can pass from brain to brain. Indeed:

> the souls of many come to take up their abode in one brain, by a natural process … the individual brain assimilates the feelings and conceptions of all its peers, in a truer sense than the body assimilates the different materials of its food. … Supposing the incorporated soul to exert an adequate influence for good on the brain in which it lives again, it shares in the immortality of that brain obtains.
>
> (SSP, IV, 91)

Long before Adorno noted the 'death of immortality' Comte had questioned it. Long before Claude Lefort wrote against Adorno, 'immortality is an attribute of figures whose words or deeds outlive their ephemeral effects, who seem, in one way or another to have helped to shape the destiny of humanity' (Lefort, 1988: 263) Comte had made it a key principle of a religion organised around the adoration of fetishes.

11

Comte's Futures

Lévi-Strauss once asked in the 1960s of the lack of awareness of Durkheim's importance: 'how are we to explain this injustice done to him, and to ourselves, if not as a minor consequence of that desperate eagerness which drives us to forget our own history, to hold it in horror …' (Lévi-Strauss, 1967: 8)? But things changed.

Before a large group standing on the pavement in front of 92, Boulevard Roosevelt, Bordeaux, on Thursday 18th May 1995, a plaque was unveiled to Emile Durkheim 'founder of French sociology'. A number of speeches were made by local dignatories and academics attending the Colloque International being held at Bordeaux in celebration of the hundredth anniversary of Durkheim's famous *The Rules of Sociological Method*. Charles-Henri Cuin who organised the conference emphasised in an interview for the local newspaper that the fame of Durkheim had had to be reinstated in Bordeaux where Durkheim had written his founding works after decades through which students had been instructed to 'forget Durkheim'.

But this very act of remembering Emile Durkheim only contradicted Durkheim's own carefully worded judgement that sociology was founded by Auguste Comte: 'It is only with Auguste Comte that the great project conceived by Saint-Simon began to become a reality … It is Comte who is the father … It was also Comte who gave it the name sociology'

(Durkheim [1915], 1975: I, 110–11; see also Heilbron, in Besnard *et al.* (eds), 1993: 59–66) and Gane, in Cuin, 1997: 31–8). But if Comte founded sociology in his *Course in Positive Philosophy* (6 vols, 1830–42) Durkheim was not even a second generation sociologist. In between Comte and Durkheim there was a generation of sociologists dominated by the names of Littré and Spencer. Emile Littré's reputation is a very famous one in France, much more venerated than Comte or Durkheim – not directly for being a Comtean sociologist, but for having written a French dictionary which became a standard reference. It should be remembered however that even the recognition now accorded to Durkheim is recent and hard won, for the centenary of Durkheim's birth, 1958, as Lévi-Strauss was to point out, 'passed almost unnoticed' – a belated commemoration was held at the Sorbonne in January, 1960 (Lévi-Strauss, 1967: 8). But today sociology likes to think of itself as beginning with Durkheim and Weber. This is to place the beginnings of sociology with the inauguration of institutionalised, university sociology. But sociology did not begin in a university; it began outside the academy, two-thirds of a century earlier and was already known throughout the world in the works of Comte, Mill, and above all Herbert Spencer, well before Durkheim was appointed to teach 'social science with pedagogy' in Bordeaux in 1887.

Norbert Elias suggested that Comte could be avoided because he was 'very likely a little mad' (Elias, 1978: 33). But there is another version given by Kolakowski:

> Some of Comte's earliest disciples held the view that his thought can be divided into two distinct stages, the first of which is the source of positivism proper, whereas the second is at least a partial negation of the first and should be regarded as an unfortunate aberration, ascribable to the fact that the great philosopher was afflicted by a recurrence of his mental illness towards the end of his life. This picture of the situation has been altered, however, by twentieth-century historians. Unlike earlier students, they find that the so-called second phase of his thought, in which he elaborated his 'religion of humanity', is a natural development from the earlier, its crowning achievement rather than any sort of falling off.
>
> (Kolakowski, 1972: 60)

In fact as this book has argued if there is continuity there is also a dramatic displacement. The later writings present very considerable problems of interpretations. On the one hand they may appear to be ludicrous as many commentators continue to say. But read not as a banal and farcical programme, but as a particular kind of theoretical challenge, they yield a curious but valuable theoretical paradox. What if Comte had actually been describing not precisely a vision of utopia, but a logical prediction of certain key characteristics of future Western culture? Expressed in a slightly modified form Comte might be read to say: the onto-theological forms are in retreat, and will ultimately be replaced by forms that are predominantly fetishistic and factishic.

The present book has quite deliberately been focused and limited in scope. It has the specific aim of reassessing the so-called law of the three states as the founding discovery of sociology not to provide an intellectual biography or a history of Comteanism. Comte claimed to have given sociology its methods, methods which enabled this discovery to be made. Many versions of the law were worked out in his writings from 1822 up till his death in 1857. In this study I have presented the main versions of the law to be found in these writings and examined what Comte thought he was doing, and what others directly and indirectly have found in his work. It may be that Comteanism is one of those citadels 'much shot at perhaps but never taken by storm, which are quietly discovered one day to be no longer inhabited' (Warnock, 1969: 8). This would of course be the most ironic outcome imaginable for Comte; and the most innocuous of all outcomes – a cadaver without a ghost. Does the ghost reside elsewhere? How could one recognise the spirit of Comte? But then things changed for Comte as well.

In 1998 I went to two International Colloques in Paris celebrating the bicentenary of the birth of Auguste Comte (1798–1857). The first, called 'Auguste Comte: Science et Politique', was held in May and organised by a philosopher (Annie Petit), and out of some twenty-five to thirty or so papers (half presented in Montpellier and half later in Paris) only one was devoted to sociology. In other words, no French sociologist actually attended the conference. Indeed I was perhaps the only sociologist there, and was, at the last moment asked to join in the final 'round table'. In November I went to Paris again for the Colloque at the Sorbonne called 'Auguste Comte et l'Idée d'une Science de l'Homme'. It was attended as far as I could see by philosophers of science and historians. There were one or two papers due to be given by sociologists. Jean-Michel Berthelot presented a paper on 'Durkheim, lecteur de Comte' which looked at the distance between them intellectually through an examination of Durkheim's references to Comte (Berthelot, in Bourdeau and Chazel, 2002: 185–206). But Raymond Boudon, who was due to speak, did not in fact attend. I seemed to be the only British sociologist present at the Paris conference. I could not be absolutely sure: there was no registration, or list of participants. The man holding a recorder aloft throughout (often mistaken for wanting to ask a question), was he perhaps British? Again the sociologists, in fact, chose to leave the bicentenary celebrations to the other disciplines.

As far as I know, the only celebration of the bicentenary of Comte's birth among sociologists in Britain was one session on Comte and contemporary sociology in a Conference held at Sussex in June 1998 (two papers: by Andrew Wernick, and myself, discussant Charles Turner). Bizarre as it may seem, both at the Paris Colloques on Comte, and at the Sussex Conference, on 'Rethinking the Social', discussion of Comte's attempt to found sociology as a science seemed intrusive on business devoted to other themes. In July 2001 there was a further, third, Colloque on Comte in France, this time at Cerisy-la-Salle, and called 'Auguste Comte Aujourd'hui' organised by Michel Bourdeau (a sociologist), with Jean-François Braunstein and Annie Petit. Here 'sociology' began to be discussed once more (and see the recent work of Karsenti (2006)).

There have been changes in the fortunes of sociology over the last forty years. Malcolm Bradbury summed it up well in 1999 a year before his death (he was commenting on his book *The History Man*, with its famous hero Howard Kirk).

> Sociology was the most fashionable, radical and popular of all subjects in the academic canon of the day. In new universities like mine it acquired special place as one of those interlocking, interdisciplinary subjects that allowed us to widen and reintegrate the great map of learning. It united philosophy, political science, anthropology, economics, history, cultural and popular studies, literature and art in a spirit of quasi-scientific objectivity. It was high theory, the most conceptual of subjects; yet it was data-based, empirical, very hands-on. It was a master subject … It was a 'value free' approach to the world, yet it was also political […] and then it began to fragment and die – not as a discipline among others, but as *the* great discipline …

Bradbury ends his piece by hailing the possible return of sociology in that sense: 'we could be entering a new golden age of sociology, [and] I shall be as delighted to hail its revival as I was sad to attend its fall'.[1]

Bradbury remembers the two sides of modern sociology, its attempt to provide a scientific methodology that was somehow both value-neutral and engaged on the one hand, and its 'great map of learning' on the other. In fact Marxism, looked at from this point of view, was narrower than Comteanism which provided an account of the sciences as part of its constituting features. The irony was that the principal target of epistemological critique in those years was 'positivism' and 'empiricism' held to be more or less the same thing (for a good attempt to clarify the differences see Bryant, 1985). But if Comte's own work seemed to be biased towards the sciences and away from literature and the arts (there are few discussions of the great novelists and artists of the revolutionary and post-revolutionary period in his writings) this was perhaps compensated for by the extraordinary impact positivism had on literature, especially in Britain where in sociology's first 'golden age' leading novelists like George Eliot, George Gissing, Thomas Hardy, and later H.G. Wells engaged with Comtean themes (see T.R. Wright (1986) and D.M. Hesse (1996)).

In the (third) 'golden age' of the 1960s it was Marxism which played this role and had such an overwhelming influence on debates. But as Marxism and Comteanism were born out of the same matrix it could be argued that the main debates in sociology were held on the terrain marked out by the meeting point not just of 'Saint-Simon I' and political economy and Hegelian philosophy (out of which came Marxism) but also 'Saint-Simon II', and Parisian science of 1800, and Humean philosophy (out of which came Comtean sociology). The 1960s was a golden age not just of sociology but also of epistemology and the philosophy and history of science. If the debates between Popper (1961), Kuhn (1962), Laudan (1971) and Feyerabend (1981) ignited around the natural sciences they also impinged on the social sciences and towards Marx and Comte in particular. In the 1840s–1860s the debates had, in a similar way, also raged in philosophy and epistemology particularly around Comte's programme. On the one hand there were keen supporters of the new ideas like J.S. Mill and George H. Lewes (partner of George Eliot). Ranged against them were the representatives of a new kind of history of science led by William Whewell, Master of Trinity College, Cambridge. Drawn into the debates were scientists like Darwin, and philosophers like Thomas Huxley. It was in these early years that basic terms such as 'scientist' (Whewell) but also related concepts like 'agnostic' (Huxley) were coined. One might say that in the first golden age of epistemology in this sense the basic issue concerned the nature of the revolutionary transition of a discipline into scientific practices. In the second, the debates not only focused on that issue (and the role of methodology) but also on the turbulent history of established sciences which seemed to undergo further revolutions or paradigm shifts (Kuhn's 1962 book was called *The Structure of Scientific Revolutions*), and whose 'progress' could not be assured in any simple fashion any more (Fuller, 1997). In France the influence of positivism was highly significant as a stimulant amongst certain sections of the scientists (for instance in biology), and in the tradition of epistemology a 'positivism nouveau' was proposed around 1900 by Gaston Milhaud to take into account recent transformations in science, and to add a fourth to the law of the three states (see A Brenner, *in* Bourdeau *et al.* (eds), 2003: 49–63). In the twentieth century the progress of biology, and the genetic revolution that followed, delivered no benefits that were somehow free of moral dilemmas: from nineteenth-century certainties came shifts into radical (metaphysical) uncertainty.

Comte's own work ended in 1857 having just announced the definitive arrival of the positive stage and leaving it to his followers to chart its development. In fact the positive polity did not make its appearance and the followers of Comte have never been able to establish an account of what happened to the metaphysical polity after Comte's death. The official Comteans fell into the trap of thinking the positive stage had arrived and all they had to do was to proselytise the Religion of Humanity and chart the final triumphs of science. The radical secular positivists who broke with Comte for the main worked towards an accommodation with democratic institutions abandoning the law of the three states as a prejudice of its author. Comtean sociology, as Durkheim said, became sterile. And wherever it was seriously taken up it had a disastrous effect on the development of the sciences (they stood still), and the social sciences (they repeated the formulas).

In the light of this history, it might be that Comtean theory is not only a displaced sociological paradigm, but that its methods and its account of science might also be said to be justly consigned to history – not just the result of advancement in any progressive discipline, but because there was a fatal flaw in the conception of the sociocratic project itself. This raises the problem of the status of the social sciences, since although they appear to make some sort of 'progress' and there do appear to be something like 'paradigm struggles' they have not attained the status of pure science in the Kuhnian sense. It has remained a contested domain, not just in the sense that no one scientific paradigm has unambiguously triumphed, but because a substantial proportion of those engaged in the social sciences believes that the scientific model is entirely inappropriate to the analysis of culture and society (a view held by William Whewell in the nineteenth-century debates, and Anthony Giddens today). It might well be then that we are concerned not with pure sciences or with literature as such but, as Dilthey pointed out at the end of the nineteenth century (1988: 77), and Lepenies (1988) more recently, something in-between, and with what has been called a 'third curriculum' in which sociology is recognised as being a 'multi-paradigm science' (Ritzer, 2001: 58–78).

Is this a situation to be regretted? Not necessarily, for as Weber pointed out, most of the issues that fall under this rubric, which might be called the zone of metaphysics, have to be faced ethically and politically. Thus it is possible and indeed necessary to turn the later against early Foucault.

The early Foucault, criticising Comte, calls 'anthropologisation' that situation where well founded knowledge (language, life, production), when subject to 'the slightest deviation from ... rigorously defined plans sends thought tumbling over into the domain occupied by the human sciences ... 'Anthropologisation' is the great internal *threat* to knowledge in our day' (1970: 348, my emphasis). The impression of 'haziness, inexactitude, and imprecision left by almost all the human sciences is merely a surface effect of what makes it possible to define them in their positivity' (p. 355). In other words unlike all the other sciences, the 'human sciences' do not have their own true objects but are 'sciences of duplication, in a "meta-epistemological" position in respect to existing sciences' (p. 355). For Baudrillard (1994) this is precisely the zone of 'simulacra'. Foucault during the period of high rationalism, defined this space negatively and with contempt. He came to reverse this judgement however and to see it is precisely in that zone, once called 'metaphysics', in which new kinds of problems concerning the transformation of human values (including human freedom) are encountered and assessed. They are problems where those involved may not be able to be aware of the consequences of action, but where it is possible to choose and act not out of 'conviction' but out of 'responsibility'. The problem of deciding what is currently known runs into the problem pursued most cogently by Foucault in his examination not of epistemology as such, but of the relation between power and knowledge, and the problem of *parrhesia* (see the writings of the last period of Foucault's life, for example, *Fearless Speech* ([1983] 2001)).

It would seem that this continent, half-science and half-humanities, might be described in Comtean terms as a zone of 'intellectual' contestation par excellence, occupied today for the moment by shifting compromises which locate themselves within the wider metaphysical polity resulting from the struggle between theologies and sciences on the one hand and between power interests and technological 'progression' on the other. According to Steve Fuller it is not positivism but 'Bioliberalism [that] is the biggest threat to the social sciences' (2006: 12). Today Comte's conception of humanity can provide the basis for a sociological defence of the idea of society against a new biological reductionism. But at what cost? For Comte, in founding sociology, produced both a classic theory of the dynamics of modernity and new challenging perspectives that revealed this theory's radical limitations.

Glossary

Altruism This word was coined by Comte and was adopted immediately and widely, and came to be used as the opposite pole of action to that of egoism. 'Live for others' became Comte's extreme altruistic motto.

Fetishism A concept which Comte adopted positively unlike Marx, designating the earliest and eternal cultural formation in which the object world is both living and worshipped.

Humanity The object of worship of the Religion of Humanity conceived as the totality of the highest representatives of humankind. Humanity is the real object actually worshipped by all religions.

Law Scientific law is a verifiable proposition in which an invariant structure permits degrees of variation of its elements in a determinable manner.

Metaphysics A central term in Comte's theory which designates a prolongation of theology into a realm of secular hidden and unverifiable causation.

Method For Comte method is defined in the widest manner, the whole research process: theory, observation, logic of analysis, forms of exposition. It can be of two kinds, objective or subjective.

Ontology Term used to describe how hidden metaphysical beings and objects are produced.

Order Hierarchical arrangement of elements into a coherent viable system whether social or intellectual, even where there are incompatible components.

Positivism Comte coined this concept to designate a particular kind of philosophy that plays the role of classifying and organising the system of the sciences and eventually the 'spiritual' order of the social system, and thereby the entire hierarchy of the social and industrial economy.

Positive order This order includes the sciences and industry and all the sites in society and culture where the processes of constructive reason are at work.

Progress The driving force of history only occurs in the rising positive order, not in theology or metaphysics. Progression is the successful application of reason.

Religion This term changed meaning in Comte's work and came to be distinguished from theology and fetishism to mean the activity of creating and recreating social and intellectual unity in society though the impulses of sympathy.

Sociology Comte coined this word to designate the application of positive methods to the study of society. He conceived it as located in the system of the sciences but with its own distinctive methods and theoretical objects.

Spiritual power As distinct from the temporal power, spiritual power is the realm of objective and subjective speculation, ideas, science and moral authority.

Subjectivity The pure imagination aided by (forms) images and signs that can pass from body to body.

Theology In the first half of Comte's work included fetishism, polytheism and monotheism as religious systems of thought, but in later work it came to include polytheistic and monotheistic religions of hidden spirits and gods.

Theory The crucial action of the abstract imagination in a science or speculative thought that coherently directs inquiry and explanation.

Notes

1 AN INTRODUCTION TO COMTE'S IDEAS

1 Notably Mary Pickering, 1993.

2 In the crisis of the insurrection in Paris in June 1848, Comte wrote a 'Saint Clotilde', an address of commemoration on the anniversary of Clotilde's death. In the address he referred to the 'ill-omened detonations … of the bloody conflict' going on around him. He said:

> I am indebted to thee for finding some pure satisfaction in a dreadful crisis … Though mingled with warlike sounds, I already hear indications that the human metropolis is returning to its normal condition. The carnage on both sides may have ceased, at least until the next conflict, which will be still more terrible, unless the working men now in arms shall have discovered their real camp.

A. Comte, *Confessions and Testament: And his Correspondence with Clotilde de Vaux*, edited by A. Crompton (Liverpool, 1910): 349–57. On Comte in 1848, see Pickering (1999) and Aron (1965).

3 Comte might well have been influenced by the revival of Catholicism which emphasised Christian love. See a discussion of this in

E. Berenson, 'A New Religion of the Left: Christianity and Social Radicalism in France, 1815–48', in *The French Revolution and the Creation of Modern Political Culture*, edited by F. Furet and M. Ozouf (Oxford, 1989), vol. 3, Chapter 29. For the details of Comte's religious practice see for example the collection of texts in The Religion of Humanity, edited by A. Crompton (Liverpool, 1907).

4 Comte, System, vol. IV, p. 212. For a discussion of this point see Sarah Kofman, *Aberrations: Le Devenir Femme d'Auguste Comte* (Paris, 1978: 159–71).

5 The reading of Soviet communism as a realisation of Comteanism is given in R. Debray, *Critique of Political Reason* (London, 1983), pp. 228–33.

6 For a stimulating attempt to discuss this with reference to the French case see Louis Dumont, 'Left versus Right in French Political Ideology', in *Transition to Modernity* (Cambridge, 1992) edited by J.A. Hall and I.C. Jarvie, pp. 259–80.

7 Aron (1965), Manuel (1962), Popper (1961), Hayek (1952), Elias (1978), Evans-Pritchard (1970). And we should add Fletcher (1966), Charlton (1959), Simon (1963).

8 Wright (1986), Pickering (1993), Hesse (1996), Scharff (1995) Harp (1995), Wernick (2001).

2 THE COMTEAN ILLUSION

1 T. Dixon, 'The invention of altruism: Auguste Comte's positive polity and respectable unbelief in Victorian Britain', in Knight and Eddy, 2005.

2 These writers have direct or indirect links with Comte. Musil wrote a doctoral thesis on positive philosophy, and his novel *Man Without Qualities* (1930–43) can be read as a Comtean portrayal of identity without selfhood; Hermann Hesse essayed his own three state law (Ziolkowski, in Hesse, 1990: xiii), as did H.G. Wells in *A Modern Utopia* ([1905] 2005); Dali imagined the surrealist movement organized along Comtean lines (1966); and Michel Houellebecq on Comte (in Bourdeau *et al.*, 2003: 7–12).

3 Althusser acknowledged the importance of Comte's distinction between the historical order of a science's formation and the order of its doctrine (in Macherey, 1964: 52). Comte also theorised the idea of the order of exposition of a scientific doctrine, and came close to formulating the principles of structural causation so central to Althusserian epistemology. And this should not be surprising since Althusser was decisively influenced by the work of Gaston Bachelard

(1968), described by Serres as 'Comte among us' (in Comte, 1975: I, 4). The central idea of the 'epistemological break', that is the thesis that all sciences are formed in a break with ideological knowledge, an idea central to the French tradition of historical epistemology (Heilbron, 1995: 262–6), is essentially a reading of Comte's law of the three states as a law of scientific revolution. And just as Comte argued for a crucial role of scientific philosophy in the formation and control of the methods of a new science, Althusser said if 'philosophy always arrives *post festum*' (1972: 166–7): it is the role of that philosophy to recover a science that has for the moment become blocked. One of the terms Althusser used for his activities in theory was involution – improving one part of Marxism from developments in another (1990). For another kind of analysis see 'Comte and Marx' pp.19–53, in S. Seidman, *Contested Knowledge; Social Theory in the Postmodern Era*, Blackwell, 1994).

4 One way of thinking about this is via Althusser and Balibar's own notion of theoretical problematic and its relationship to a theoretical discursive field. For example their analysis of historicism as a problematic led them to suggest that when Sartre, who used the historicist method, came into contact with Marxism he 'immediately gave an historicist reading of it' just as Gramsci had done (but from another tradition) (1970: 135). The historicist reading of Marxism produces effects through its notions of time, linearity, and so on in relation to the materials provided by Marxism itself, some of which may well have been historicist in Althusser's sense. I say in Althusser's sense because it was one of the major points of latent disagreement between Derrida and Althusser that the critique of historicism is made paradoxically by Sartre's mentor, Husserl against Dilthey at the beginning of the century. Althusser's refusal to acknowledge this says Derrida 'irritated me even if I understood, without approving of it, the political strategy involved' (in Kaplan, 1993: 192). But what I am suggesting, using Althusser against himself here (but in a different direction for the moment from that of Derrida), is that at base, Marxism itself is only one variation of a much richer deeper (Saint-Simonianism) matrix crucially involving the materials with which Comte also worked – because he was involved in constructing it. So when Althusser encountered Marx's version of the Saint-Simonian matrix Althusser produced a structuralist reading of it, just as Comte in fact had done over 100 years before. Now the latter was not a 'bourgeois' reading as most Marxists have asserted. We know that Comte associated the bourgeoisie with metaphysical philosophy and its polity (parliamentary democracy). Comte's own

position was essentially one which advocated the anti-bourgeois alliance: patrician, proletarian, neo-papal – not a fascism which is caesaro-patrician-proletarian. Althusser's own ideal was certainly anti-bourgeois, proletarian, communist, but its precise political form always remained undefined. Wernick's recent insightful reading suggests that Althusser was led 'to think Lenin's 'vanguard party' – the locus of fusion between intellectuals and militants, theory and practice, science and politics – into the space of Comte's revamped *pouvoir spirituel*' (2001: 235, emphasis in original).

5 Edward O. Wilson (2005) *New Scientist*, 5 November: 48–9. Steve Fuller's recent book (2006) appeals to 'Humanity' as an 'endangered species'.

3 THE CONTEXT AND MATERIALS OF SOCIOLOGY

1 There is a long running debate about how to translate Comte's French terms, *lois des trois états*: should this be law of three stages or three states? In this book I have chosen 'three states' as Comte himself could certainly have used another French term if he had wanted to signal stages (*étapes*). On the law of the three states itself the following cover the range of commentaries: Harrison (1913), Ginsberg (1956), Hobhouse (1966), Cohen (1965), Laudan (1971), Scharff (1995), Schmauss (1982). Rickert (1986) represents another kind of assessment, beyond Comte and Hegel (and we might add Marx) that finds these writers 'defenceless' against modern epistemological criticism: can there be 'laws of history'?

4 THE INTIMATIONS OF SOCIAL SCIENCE AND A NEW POLITICS

1 Durkheim tried to clarify the rules governing the analysis of abnormal forms and to define social dysfunction and teratology. Durkheim insisted the norm was always the norm of a particular species at a certain stage of its development. He went on to add that there were pathologies of function (physiological dysfunctions), and pathologies of structure (malformations and teratologies). Pain itself is not an indication of pathology (the pains of childbirth for instance are not abnormal). This kind of approach, and it reaches its high point with Durkheim, is nothing more than the application of certain highly abstract and formal ways of thinking about pathology applied to social phenomena. It establishes the claim that social science should aim to be therapeutic in its ambitions, for 'disease has a greater

place in human societies than anywhere else' (Durkheim [1892] 1997: 56e). If this position remained formal it was in anticipation that the social sciences would be able in the future to identify an immense field of pathological phenomena in an adequate conceptualisation.

The general field of 'abnormal forms' or pathology in the analysis of social life fell into decline after Durkheim and was abandoned in favour of the study of social 'deviance'. The very idea of a study of social pathology itself was critiqued by Szasz and Foucault in particular as a new form of power which came into existence at the end of the eighteenth century as an essential component of the 'disciplinary' society. Foucault was himself clearly indebted to Canguilhem and he made this evident himself on several occasions, such as his lectures at the Collège de France (2003). Thus while the field of pathology and abnormal forms continues in psychology it has been abandoned in sociology, leaving only traces (such as the concept of 'anomie') in the works of some thinkers such as Baudrillard, whose usage may be ironic more than an attempt to revive the terrain. Foucault seems to approach a position elaborated in sociology earlier by Max Weber in his rejection of the attempt to use the field of pathology as a way of evading moral choices. The fundamental issues posed by the project of social science continue to be haunted by the same set of problems as established in analysis of pathological phenomena whether it be conceived in terms of order and 'disorder' (chaos), social breakdown, radical evil, 'failed states', even deviation or non-compliance with 'correct' forms of language or behaviour (harassment, racism, child abuse, etc.) and so on, or pathology (perversion, dysfunction, disease, illness, abnormalities). The question in part is: is there anything lost by replacing pathology with more political, religious, moral, and legal terminologies? From Foucault's point of view of course what is lost is a modern power tactic: redefinition 'rogue' states as pathological with the ancient religious language of 'axis of evil' is a return to pre-modern form of spectacular sanction (techniques of public torture).

6 BUT WHY DID COMTE NEED SOCIOLOGY?

1 In one of Comte's humorous asides – a tendency to eat more, or eat less must not be assumed to be absolute. This rests also on the principle that social development does not create new faculties; all the essential dispositions for such development exist as a germ in the primary state (1974b: 153).

2 Althusser commented on the epistemology of this basically essentialist procedure that 'Michelangelo developed a whole aesthetic of artistic production based not on the production of the essential form out of the marble but on the destruction of the non-form which envelops the form to be disengaged even before the first chip is cut' (in Althusser and Balibar, 1970: 37).

9 A SECOND SOCIOLOGY

1 Canguilhem has written an excellent essay on the concept of fetishism (1968: 81–98). This essay considers the sources of the idea of fetishism, but was never connected to a sociology or theory of religion. Whenever Canguilhem approaches Comte's sociology it is to stress Comte's purely evaluative idea of a normal social state as one characterised by harmonic consensus of its parts. While he is in fact highly respectful of Comte's thought, defending the rational opposition to cell theory (1975: 64–6), and his support of phrenology (1983: 268), Canguilhem like Whewell stops well short of a discussion of the main elements of Comte's sociological analyses, and the law of the three states as such.

10 SOCIOLOGISTS AND THE REGIME OF FETISHES

1 'A cult of man is quite different from egoistic individualism', because the individual in Durkheim's sociology has deep subjectivity and human rights (Durkheim 1970: 336–7).

2 A recurrent theme in Comte's reflections: where do the gods reside?

11 COMTE'S FUTURES

1 Bradbury, M. (1999) *Sunday Times*, 3 January.

Bibliography

Acton, H. B. (1974) *The Idea of a Spiritual Power*. London: Athlone.

Althusser, L. (1972) *Montesquieu, Rousseau, Marx*. London: Verso.

Althusser, L. (1990) *Philosophy and the Spontaneous Philosophy of the Scientists*. London: Verso.

Althusser, L. (1997) *The Spectre of Hegel: Early Writings*. London: Verso.

Althusser, L. and Balibar, E. (1970) *Reading Capital*. London: NLB.

Aron, R. (1965) *Main Currents in Sociological Thought*, vol. 1. Harmondsworth: Penguin.

Bachelard, G. (1968) *The Philosophy of No*. New York: Orion.

Barthes, R. (1976) *Sade, Loyola, Fourier*. New York: Hill and Wang.

Baudrillard, J. (1988) *The Ecstasy of Communication*. New York: Semiotext(e).

Baudrillard, J. (1993) *Symbolic Exchange and Death*. London: Sage.

Baudrillard, J. (1994) *Simulacra and Simulation*. Ann Arbor, MI: University of Michigan Press.

Bensaude-Vincent, B. (1991) 'L'astronomie populaire, priorité philosophique et projet politique', *Revue de Synthèse*, 1: 49–60.

Bensaude-Vincent, B. (1999) 'Atomism and Positivism: A Legend about French Chemistry', *Annals of Science*, 56, 1: 81–94.

Berenson, E. (1989) 'A New Religion of the Left: Christianity and Social Radicalism in France, 1815–48', in F. Furet and M. Ozouf (eds) *The French Revolution and the Creation of Modern Political Culture*. Oxford: Pergamon Press, vol. 3, ch. 29.

Berthelot, J.-M. (1991) *La Construction de la Sociologie*. Paris: Presses Universitaires de France.

Besnard, P., Borlandi, M. and Vogt, P. (eds) (1993) *Division de Travail et Lien Social*. Paris: Presses Universitaires de France.

Boudon, R. (2004) *The Poverty of Relativism*. Oxford: Bardwell Press.

Bourdeau, M. and Chazel, F. (eds) (2002) *Auguste Comte et l'Idée de Science de l'Homme*. Paris: L'Harmattan.

Bourdeau, M., Braunstein, J.-F. and Petit, A. (eds) (2003) *Auguste Comte Aujourd'hui*. Paris: Kimé.

Bradbury, M. (1999) 'Return of the History Man', *Sunday Times*, 3 January: section 2, p. 5.

Braunstein, J.-F. (2003) 'La Religion des Morts-Vivants: Le Culte des Morts Chez Auguste Comte', *Revue des Sciences Philosophiques et Théologiques*, 87: 59–73.

Brooks, J. (1998) *The Eclectic Legacy: Academic Philosophy and the Human Sciences in Nineteenth Century France*. London: Associated University Presses.

Brown, R. (1997) 'Artificial Experiments on Society: Comte, G.C. Lewis and Mill', *Journal of Historical Sociology*, 10, 1: 74–97.

Bryant, C.G. (1985) *Positivism in Social Theory and Research*. Basingstoke: Macmillan.

Canguilhem, G. (1968) *Etudes d'Histoire et de la Philosophie des Sciences*. Paris: Vrin.

Canguilhem, G. (1975) *La Connaissance de la Vie*. Paris: Vrin.

Canguilhem, G. (1981) *Idéologie et Rationalité dans l'Histoire des Sciences de Vie*. Paris: Vrin.

Canguilhem, G. (1988) *Ideology and Rationality in the History of the Life Sciences*. Cambridge, MA: MIT Press.

Canguilhem, G. (1989) *The Normal and the Pathological*. New York: Zone

Canguilhem, G. (1994) *A Vital Rationalist, Selected Writings from Georges Canguilhem*. New York: Zone.

Canguilhem, G. (1998) 'The Decline of the Idea of Progress', *Economy and Society*, 27, 2&3: 313–29.

Charlton, D.G. (1959) *Positivist Thought in France During the Second Empire*. Westport, CT: Greenwood.

Charlton, D.G. (1963) *Secular Religions in France, 1815–1870*. London: Oxford University Press.

Charlton, D.G. (1974) 'French Thought in the Nineteenth and Twentieth Centuries', in D.C. Potts and D.G. Charlton (eds) *French Thought Since 1600*. London: Methuen, pp. 41–86.

Clauzade, L. (1996) Le Statut Philosophique des Communes médiévales chez Saint-Simon, A. Thierry et A. Comte', *Cahiers de Recherches Médiévales*, 2: 97–107.

Cohen, D. (1965) 'Comte's Changing Sociology', *American Journal of Sociology*, lxxi: 168–77.

Cohen, P. (1980) 'Is Positivism Dead?', *Sociological Review*, 28, 1: 141–76.

Comte, A. (1851) *The Philosophy of Mathematics*. New York: Harper and Brothers.

Comte, A. (1889) *Appeal to Conservatives*. London: Trubner.

Comte, A. (1891a) *The Catechism of Positivism*. London: Trubner.

Comte, A. (1891b) *Subjective Synthesis*. London: Kegan Paul, Trench, Trubner.

Comte, A. (1903) *A Discourse on the Positive Spirit*. London: Reeves.

Comte, A. (1907) *The Religion of Humanity*. Liverpool: Church of Humanity.

Comte, A. (1910) *Confessions and Testament: And his Correspondence with Clotilde de Vaux*, edited by A. Crompton. Liverpool, pp 349–57.

Comte, A. (1968) *A System of Positive Polity*, 4 vols [London, 1877] reprinted in New York.

Comte, A. (1970) *Introduction to Positive Philosophy*. Indianapolis, IN: Bobbs-Merrill.

Comte, A. (1974a) *Crisis of Industrial Civilization*. London: Heinemann.

Comte, A. (1974b) *The Positive Philosophy*. New York: AMS Press.

Comte, A. (1974c) *The Essential Comte*, edited by S. Andreski. London: Croom Helm.

Comte, A. (1975) *Cours de Philosophie Positive*, 2 vols. Paris. Hermann.

Comte, A. (1998) *Early Political Writings*, edited by H.S. Jones. Cambridge: Cambridge University Press.

Cooter, R.J. (1976) 'Phrenology: the Provocation of Progress', *History of Science*, 14: 211–34.

Cuin, C.-H. (ed.) (1997) *Durkheim d'un Siècle a l'Autre*. Paris: Presses Universitaires de France.

Cunliffe, J. and Reeve, A. (1996) 'Exploitation: the Original Saint-Simonian Account', *Capital and Class*, 59: 61–80.

Dagognet, F. (1997) Georges Canguilhem, Philosophe de la Vie. Le Plessis-Robinson: Synthelabo.

Dali, S. (1966) *Diary of a Genius*. London: Hutchinson.
Debray, R. (1983) *Critique of Political Reason*. London: Verso.
Dijkstra, B. (1986) *Idols of Perversity*. Oxford: Oxford University Press.
Dilthey, W. (1988) *Introduction to the Human Sciences*. London: Harvester Wheatsheaf.
Durkheim, E. (1962) *Socialism and Saint-Simon*. New York: Collier.
Durkheim, E. (1964) *The Division of Labour in Society*. London: Collier.
Durkheim, E. (1970) *Suicide*. London: Routledge.
Durkheim, E. (1973) *Moral Education*. London: Collier.
Durkheim, E. (1975) *Textes*, edited by V. Karady. Paris: Editions de Minuit.
Durkheim, E. (1978) *Durkheim on Institutional Analysis*, edited by M. Traugott. Chicago, IL: University of Chicago Press
Durkheim, E. (1982)*The Rules of Sociological Method*. London: Macmillan.
Eisen, S. (1967) 'Herbert Spencer and the Spectre of Comte', *Journal of British Studies*, 7: 48–67.
Elias, N. (1978) *What is Sociology*? London: Hutchinson.
Engels, F. (1943) *Anti-Dürhing*. London: Lawrence and Wishart.
Evans-Pritchard, E.E. (1970) *The Sociology of Auguste Comte: An Appreciation*. Manchester: Manchester University Press.
Ferguson, H. (ed.) (1998) *Virtual History*. London: Macmillan.
Feyerabend, P. (1981) 'More Clothes from the Emperor's Bargain Basement', *British Journal of the Philosophy of Science*, 32: 57–94.
Fishman, L. (1950) 'A pathology of Auguste Comte', *Psychoanalytic Review*, 37, I: 66–70.
Fletcher, R. (1966) *Auguste Comte and the Making of Sociology*. London: Athlone Press.
Fletcher, R. (ed.) (1974) *The Science of Society and the Unity of Mankind*. London: Heinemann.
Foucault, M. (1972) *The Archaeology of Knowledge*. London: Tavistock.
Foucault, M. (1977) *Language, Counter-Memory, Practice*. New York: Cornell.
Foucault, M. (1985) *The Use of Pleasure*. London: Penguin.
Foucault, M. (1991) *The Birth of the Clinic*. London: Routledge.
Foucault, M. (2001) *Fearless Speech*. Los Angeles: Semiotext(e).
Foucault, M. (2003) *Abnormal*. London: Verso.
Fraser, C.G. (1990) 'Lagrange's Analytical Mathematics, Its Cartesian Origins and Reception in Comte's Positive Philosophy', *Studies in History and Philosophy of Science*, 21, June: 243–56.
Friedrichs, R. (1972) *A Sociology of Sociology*. New York: Free Press.

Fuller, S. (1997) *Science*. Buckingham: Open University Press.

Fuller, S. (2006) *The New Sociological Imagination*. London: Sage.

Furedi, F. (1992) *Mythical Past, Elusive Future*. London: Pluto.

Furet, F. (1992) *Revolutionary France: 1770–1880*. Oxford: Blackwell.

Gane, M. (1993) *Harmless Lovers? Gender, Theory and Personal Relationships*. London: Routledge.

Gane, M. (1995) 'Unresolved Comte', *Economy and Society*, 4,1: 138–49.

Gane, M. (1995) 'La Distinction du Normal et du Pathologique', in Borlandi *et al.* (eds) *Les Regles de la Methode Sociologique*, Paris: L'Harmattan, pp. 185–205.

Gane, M. (1997) 'Durkheim Contre Comte', in H. Cuin (ed.) *La Méthode Durkheimienne d'un Siècle a l'Autre*, Paris: Presses Universitaires de France, pp. 31–8.

Gane, M. (2003) *French Social Theory*. London: Sage.

Gane, M. (2005) 'Untamed', *The Semiotic Review of Books*, 15, 1: 7–9.

Gane, N. (2004) *The Future of Social Theory*. London: Continuum.

Gellner, E. (1985) *Relativism and the Social Sciences*. Cambridge: Cambridge University Press.

Gérard, A. ([1789] 1970) *La Revolution Française; Mythes et Interprétations*. Paris: Flammarion.

Ginsburg, M. (1956) *On the Diversity of Morals*. London: Heinemann.

Greene, J.C. (1962) 'Biology and Social Theory in the Nineteenth Century: Auguste Comte and Herbert Spencer', in M. Clagett (ed.) *Critical Problems in the History of Science*. Madison, WI: University of Wisconsin Press, pp. 419–46.

Goldstein, J. (1990) *Console and Classify: The French Psychiatric Profession in the Nineteenth Century*. Cambridge: Cambridge University Press.

Goldstein, J. (2005) *The Post-Revolutionary Self: Politics and Psyche in France, 1750–1850*. London: Harvard University Press.

Gould, S.J. (2003) *The Fox, and the Magister's Pox: Mending the Gap Between Science and the Humanities*. London: Cape.

Grange, J. (1996) *La Philosophie d'Auguste Comte: Science, Politique, Religion*. Paris: Presses Universitaires de France.

Hacking, I. (ed.) (1981) *Scientific Revolutions*. Oxford: Oxford University Press.

Hacking, I. (1990) *The Taming of Chance*. Cambridge: Cambridge University Press.

Haight, G. and Van Arsdal, R. (eds) (1982) *George Eliot: A Centenary Tribute*. Basingstoke: Macmillan.

Haines, B. (1978) 'The Inter-Relations between Social, Biological, and Medical Thought, 1750–1850: Saint-Simon and Comte', *British Journal for the History of Science*, 11, March: 19–35.

Hall, J. and Jarvie, I. (eds) (1992) *Transition to Modernity*. Cambridge: Cambridge University Press.

Harp, G. (1995) *Positivist Republic: Auguste Comte and the Reconstruction of American Liberalism, 1865–1920*. Pennsylvania: Penn State Press.

Harrison, F. (1913) 'Law of Three Stages', *Positivist Review*, 1 July: 145–51.

Harrison, R. (1959) 'E.S. Beesley and Karl Marx', *International Review of Social History*, 4: 22–58, 208–38.

Hawkins, M. (1979) 'Comte, Durkheim and the Sociology of Primitive Religion' *Sociological Review*, 27: 429–46.

Hawkins, M. (1984) 'Reason and Sense Perception in Comte's Theory of Mind', *History of European Ideas*, 5: 149–63.

Hayek, F.A. (1952) *The Counter-Revolution of Science: Studies in the Abuse of Reason*. Glencoe, IL: The Free Press.

Hayward, J. (1991) *After the French Revolution: Six Critics of Democracy and Nationalism*. New York: New York University Press.

Heilbron, J. (1990) 'Auguste Comte and Modern Epistemology', *Sociological Theory*, 8, Fall: 153–62.

Heilbron, J. (1991) 'Theory of Knowledge and Theory of Science in the Work of Auguste Comte. Note on Comte's Originality', *Revue de Synthèse*, CXII: 75–89.

Heilbron, J. (1993) 'Ce que Durkheim doit a Comte', in P. Besnard, M. Borlandi and P. Vogt (eds) *Division du Travail et Lien Social*. Paris: Presses Universitaires de France.

Heilbron, J. (1995) *The Rise of Social Theory*. Oxford: Polity Press.

Heilbron, J. (1996) 'Auguste Comte and historical epistemology: a reply to Dick Pels', *History of the Human Sciences*, 9, 2: 153–9.

Hesse, D.M. (1996) *George Eliot and Auguste Comte*. Frankfurt: Peter Lang.

Hesse, H. (1974) *If the War Goes On: Reflections on War and Politics*. London: Picador.

Hesse, H. (1990) *The Glass Bead Game*. London: Owl Books.

Hobbes, T. (1946) *Leviathan*. Oxford: Blackwell.

Hobhouse, L.T. (1966) *Sociology and Philosophy*. London: Bell.

Horkheimer, M. (1972) *Critical Theory*. New York: Continuum.

Iggers, G. (ed.) (1972) *The Doctrine of Saint-Simon: An Exposition*. New York: Schocken.

Kaplan, E. *et al.* (eds) (1993) *The Althusserian Legacy*. London: Verso.
Karsenti, B. (2006) *Politique de l'Esprit: Auguste Comte et la Naissance de la Science Sociale*. Paris: Hermann.
Kemple, T. (2004) 'L'Effet Comte', *Journal of Classical Sociology*, 4, 3: 361–82.
Kent, C. (1978) *Brains and Numbers: Elitism, Comtism and Democracy in Mid-Victorian England*. Toronto: University of Toronto Press.
Knight, D. and Eddy, M. (2005) *Science and Beliefs*. Aldershot: Ashgate.
Knights, B. (1978) *The Idea of the Clerisy in the Nineteenth Century*. Cambridge: Cambridge University Press.
Kofman, S. (1978) *Aberrations: Le Devenir Femme d'Auguste Comte*. Paris: Aubier-Flammarion.
Kolakowski, L. (1972) *Positivist Philosophy*. London: Penguin.
Kremer-Marietti, A. (1982) *Entre le Signe et l'Histoire: L'Anthropologie d'Auguste Comte*. Paris: Klincksieck.
Kuhn, T. (1962) *The Structure of Scientific Revolutions*. Chicago, IL: University of Chicago Press.
Lahire, B. (2005) *L'Esprit Sociologique*. Paris: Découverte.
Latour, B. (1996) *Petite Réflexion sur le Culte Moderne de Dieux Faitiches*. Le Plessis-Robinson: Synthélabo.
Latour, B. (1999) *Pandora's Hope*. London: Harvard University Press.
Laudan, L. (1971) 'Towards a Reassessment of Comte's "Methode Positive"', *Philosophy of Science*, 38, March: 35–53.
Lefort, C. (1988) *Democracy and Political Theory*. Oxford: Polity Press.
Lepenies, W. (1988) *Between Literature and Science: The Rise of Sociology*. Cambridge: Cambridge University Press.
Lévi-Strauss, L. (1967) *The Scope of Anthropology*. London: Cape.
Lévi-Strauss, L. (1972) *The Savage Mind*. London: Weidenfeld and Nicholson
Lewisohn, D. (1972) 'Mill and Comte on the Methods of Social Science', *Journal of the History of Ideas*, 33: 315–24.
Littré, E. (1864) *Auguste Comte et la Philosophie Positive*. Paris: Hachette.
Littré, E. (1879) *Conservation, Révolution et Positivisme*, 2nd edn. Paris: Bureaux de la Philosophy Positive.
Lockwood, D. (1982) 'Fatalism: Durkheim's hidden theory of order', in A. Giddens and G. MacKenzie (eds) *Social Class and the Division of Labour*. Cambridge: Cambridge University Press, pp. 101–18.
Lyotard, J.-F. (1984) *The Postmodern Condition*. Manchester: Manchester University Press.
Macherey, P. (1964) 'La Philosophie de la Science de Georges Canguilhem', *La Pensée*, 113: 50–74.

Macherey, P. (1989) *Comte: La Philosophie et les Sciences*. Paris: Presses Universitaires de France.
Maffesoli, M. (1993) *The Shadow of Dionysus: A Contribution to the Sociology of the Orgy*. New York: State University of New York Press.
Manuel, F. (1956) *The New World of Henri Saint-Simon*. Cambridge, MA: Harvard University Press.
Manuel, F. (1962) *The Prophets of Paris*. New York: Harper and Row.
Marx, K. (1971) *A Contribution to the Critique of Political Economy*. London: Lawrence and Wishart.
Marx, K. (1979) *The Letters of Karl Marx*, edited by S. Padover. New York: Prentice-Hall.
Marx, K. and Engels, F. (1975) *Collected Works*, vol 3. London: Lawrence and Wishart.
McCormick, M.A. (1974) 'Tissue Theory in Auguste Comte's Positive Biology', *Texas Reports on Biology and Medicine*, 32, 1: 75–87.
Mellor, P.A. (2004) *Religion, Realism and Social Theory*. London: Sage.
Milbank, J. (1993) *Theology and Social Theory*. Oxford: Blackwell.
Mill, J.S. (1961) *Auguste Comte and Positivism*. Ann Arbor, MI: University of Michigan Press.
Mill, J.S. (1988) *The Logic of the Moral Sciences*. La Salle, PA: Open Court.
Mommsen, W. and Osterhammel, J. (eds) (1987) *Max Weber and his Contemporaries*. London: Unwin Hyman.
Moses, C.G. (1982) 'Saint-Simonian Men/Saint-Simonian Women', *Journal of Modern History*, 54, June: 240–67.
Moses, C.G. and Rabine, L.W. (1993) *Feminism, Socialism and French Romanticism*. Bloomington, IN: Indiana University Press.
Muglioni, J. (1995) *Auguste Comte*. Paris: Kimé.
Nietzsche, F. (1982) *Daybreak*. Cambridge: Cambridge University Press.
Nisbet, R.A. (1967) *The Sociological Tradition*. London: Heinemann.
Nye, R. (1982) 'Heredity, Pathology and Psychoneurosis in Durkheim's Early Work', *Knowledge and Society*, 4: 103–42.
Nye, R. (1998) *Masculinity and Male Codes of Honour in Modern France*. Berkeley, CA: University of California Press.
Peirce, C.S. (1982) *Collected Papers*, vol. 1. Indiana: Indiana University Press.
Petit, A. (1991) 'La revolution occidental selon Auguste Comte: Entre l'histoire et l'utopie', *Revue de Synthèse*, Jan–March: 21–40.
Petit, A. (ed.) (2003) *Auguste Comte: Trajectoires Positivistes, 1798–1998*. Paris: L'Harmattan.

Pickering, M. (1993) *Auguste Comte: An Intellectual Biography*, vol. 1, Cambridge, Cambridge University Press.

Pickering, M. (1996) 'Angels and Demons in the Moral Vision of Auguste Comte', *Journal of Women's History*, 8: 10–40.

Pickering, M. (1997a) 'A New Look at Auguste Comte', in C. Camic (ed.) *Reclaiming the Sociological Classics: The State of the Scholarship*. Oxford: Blackwell, pp. 11–44.

Pickering, M. (1997b) 'Rhetorical Strategies in the Works of Auguste Comte', in *Historical Reflections/Reflexions Historiques*, 23, 2: 151–57.

Pickering, M. (1998) 'Auguste Comte and the Return to Primitivism', *Revue Internationale de Philosophie*, 203: 51–77.

Pickering, M. (1999) 'Auguste Comte and the Revolution of 1848', *Proceedings of the Consortium on Revolutionary Europe 1750–1850*, pp. 464–76.

Pickering, M. (2000) 'Clotilde de Vaux and the Search for Identity', in J.B. Margadant (ed.) *The New Biography: Performing Femininity in the nineteenth-century*. Berkeley, CA: University of California Press.

Pilbeam, P. (2000a) *French Socialists Before Marx*. Teddington: Acumen.

Pilbeam, P. (2000b) 'Dream Worlds? Religion and the Early Socialists in France', *The Historical Journal*, 43, 2: 499–515.

Popper, K. (1961) *The Poverty of Historicism*. London: Routledge & Kegan Paul.

Radcliffe, B. (1973) 'Some Jewish Problems in the Early Careers of Emile and Isaac Pereire', *Jewish Social Studies*, 34, 3: 189–206.

Ranulf, S. (1939) 'Scholarly Forerunners of Fascism', *Ethics*, 50: 16–34.

Ray, L. (1999) *Theorising Classical Sociology*. Buckingham: Open University Press.

Renan, E. (1890) *L'Avenir de la Science: Pensées de 1848*. Paris: Calmann-Levy.

Renard, G. (1996) *L'Epistemologie Chez Georges Canguilhem*. Paris: Nathan.

Rey, A. (1971) 'La Theorie Positive des Langages: Comte et la Semiotique', *Semiotica*, pp. 52–74.

Rickert, H. (1986) *The Limits of Concept Formation in Natural Science*. Cambridge: Cambridge University Press.

Ritzer, G. (1996) *Sociological Theory*. London: McGraw-Hill.

Ritzer, G. (2001) *Explorations in Social Theory: From Metatheorizing to Rationalization*. London: Sage.

Ritzer, G. and Goodman, D.J. (2004) *Classical Social Theory*. London: McGraw-Hill.

Rose, G. (1984) *Dialectic of Nihilism: Post-Structuralism and Law*. Oxford: Blackwell.

Rousseau, J.-J. (1968) *The Social Contract*. Harmondsworth: Penguin.

Runciman, W.G. (1983) *A Treatise on Social Theory, vol 1: The Methodology of Social Theory*. Cambridge: Cambridge University Press.

Said, E. (1984) *The World, the Text, and the Critic*. London: Faber & Faber.

Saint-Simon, H. (1964) *Social Organisation, The Science of Man and Other Writings*, edited by F. Markham. New York, Harper.

Saint-Simon, H. (1975) *Henri Saint-Simon (1750–1825)*, edited by K. Taylor. London: Croom Helm.

Saint-Simon, H. (1976) *The Political Thought of Saint-Simon*, edited by G. Ionescu. Oxford: Oxford University Press.

Scharff, R. (1991) 'Monitoring Self-Activity: the Status of Reflection before and after Comte', *Metaphilosophy*, 22, 4: 333–48.

Scharff, R. (1995) *Comte After Positivism*. Cambridge: Cambridge University Press.

Schluchter, W. (1996) *Paradoxes of Modernity: Culture and Conduct in the Theory of Max Weber*. Stanford, CA: Stanford University Press.

Schmaus, W. (1982) 'A Reappraisal of Comte's Three-state Law', *History and Theory*, 21, 2: 248–66.

Schmaus, W. (1985) 'Hypotheses and Historical Analysis in Durkheim's Sociological Methodology: A Comtean Tradition', *Studies in History and Philosophy of Science*, 6, March: 1–30.

Seidentop, L. (1979) 'Two Liberal Traditions', in A. Ryan (ed.) *The Idea of Freedom*. Oxford: Oxford University Press, pp. 153–74.

Seidman, S. (1994) *Contested Knowledge: Social Theory in the Postmodern Era*. Oxford: Blackwell.

Serres, M. (1995) *The Natural Contract*. Ann Arbor, MI: University of Michigan Press.

Serres, M. (ed.) (1995) *A History of Scientific Thought*. Oxford: Blackwell.

Serres, M. (1997) *The Troubadour of Knowledge*. Ann Arbor, MI: University of Michigan Press.

Serres, M. and Latour, B. (1996) *Conversations on Science, Culture and Time*. Ann Arbor, MI: University of Michigan Press.

Sernin, A. (1985) *Alain: Un Sage Dans La Cité*. Paris: Laffont.

Shilling, C. and Mellors, P. (2001) *The Sociological Ambition*. London: Sage.

Simon, W.M. (1963) *European Positivism in the Nineteenth Century*. Ithaca, NY: Cornell University Press.

Sokal, A. and Bricmont, J. (1998) *Intellectual Impostures*. London: Profile Books.

Sprott, W. (1949) *Sociology*. London: Hutchinson.

Starobinski, J. (1979) *Words Upon Words: The Anagrams of Ferdinand Saussure*. New Haven, CT: Yale University Press.

Starkie, E. (1954) *Petrus Borel the Lycanthrope*. London: Faber.

Stephen, L. (1861) 'The Comtist Utopia', *Fraser's Magazine*, 80: 1–21.

Thomas à Kempis (1977) *The Imitation of Christ*. London: Fount.

Uta, M. (1928) *La Loi des Trois Etats dans la Philosophie d'Auguste Comte*. Paris: Alcan.

Vernon, R. (1984) 'Auguste Comte and the Withering-Away of the State', *Journal of the History of Ideas*, 45: 549–66.

Vernon, R. (1986) 'The Political Self: Auguste Comte and Phrenology', *History of European Ideas*, 7: 271–86.

Warnock, G.J. (1969) *English Philosophy Since 1900*. London: Oxford University Press.

Wartelle, J.-C. (2005) *L'Heritage d'Auguste Comte: Histoire de 'Eglise Positiviste'*. Paris: L'Harmattan.

Wells, H.G. (2005) *A Modern Utopia*. London: Penguin.

Wernick, A. (2000) 'From Comte to Baudrillard: Socio-Theology After the End of the Social', *Theory Culture and Society*, 17, 6: 55–75.

Wernick, A. (2001) *Auguste Comte and the Religion of Humanity*. Cambridge: Cambridge University Press.

Whewell, W. (1866) 'Comte and Positivism', *MacMillan's Magazine*, March: 351–62.

Wilson, E.O. (2005) 'Can Biology do Better Than Faith?', *New Scientist*, 5 November: 48–9.

Wilson, W.O. (1998) *Concilience: The Unity of Knowledge*. London: Abacus.

Wright, T.R. (1986) *The Religion of Humanity: the Impact of Comtean Positivism on Victorian Britain*. Cambridge: Cambridge University Press.

Index